HUNT ELK

Jim Zumbo

Winchester Press
NEW WIN PUBLISHING

All photos in this book are by the author unless other-wise noted.

Library of Congress Cataloging-in-Publication Data

Zumbo, Jim.
    Hunt elk!

Includes index.
1. Elk hunting. I. Title.
SK303.Z86   1985   799.2'773'57   85-22461
ISBN 0-8329-0383-3

To Mom and Dad, without whose suppport my dreams would never have come true.

Acknowledgments

No book of this nature is possible without outside help. As such, I'd like to thank a number of people and organizations for assisting me in this project: William H. Nesbitt, administrative director of the Boone and Crocket Club, for providing information in the trophy chapter; to the Wildlife Management Institute for maps and illustrations; and to the Foundation for Rocky Mountain Elk, for providing information in the state-by-state directory.

A special thanks goes to Clare Conley, editor of *Outdoor Life* magazine, for writing the Foreword; to *Outdoor Life* magazine for allowing me to use portions of my articles already published; and to Bob Elman, my dear friend and hunting buddy, who is also consulting editor for Winchester Press, for having the tenacity to put up with my many excuses for turning this book in far past its deadline.

Contents

CHAPTER

Foreword

I don't know what you expect to read in this foreword to Jim Zumbo's elk book, but I can virtually guarantee that what you find here will not be what you expected. This is the first time I can remember having the chance to tell the real truth—to be intentionally redundant—about Jim Zumbo. I don't get that many opportunities to report what it is really like to hunt with him, and I'm not going to waste this space and your time extolling what a great elk hunter he is. If you must, go ahead and read the book. Otherwise, stick with me and get the straight story.

I have tried to recall when I first met Jim Zumbo, but my mind has completely blanked out the event, no doubt for good reasons. It only blanks out things for good reasons. For example, in response to my wife's question, "How did a lady's shoe get under the front seat of your car?" or "How could you spend $500 on just one dinner in Las Vegas?" My mind goes blank, and I know it has a good reason. Until a better analyst than Freud comes along, meeting Zumbo falls into that category.

On the other hand, Zumbo might just have jumped full-grown upon us. I don't know. Or he might have suddenly walked down from a mountaintop bearing tablets, all of which bore the same commandment: "Bayer."

What get's my goat, or elk in this case, is that Zumbo has persuaded me to write this foreword for no pay, and I am supposed to tell you what a great book it is because he knows all about elk. So I will. Zumbo's all right, I guess. But the book is just great. I have a chair at my desk that is a little low, and this book brings me up to the perfect height for typing. If you have a low chair, you really ought to buy this book.

Last year I went elk hunting with Zumbo. And I want to tell you about it. Throughout this book you will read about how difficult it is to climb mountain after mountain searching for elk. You will learn how carefully you must stalk these wary animals. You will read about the exacting placement of long shots you must make, and you will learn about how difficult it is to pack these huge animals on the backs of horses whose one goal in life is to put the permanent print of a horseshoe on your forehead.

Ah, such are the rigors that elk hunters like Zumbo eagerly endure! Well, sometimes, maybe, but not when I was bowhunting with Zumbo last year.

I want to preface this true account of a Zumbo hunt by telling you that I was the guest. A guest is a guy who wants everyone else to help him get his elk. I claimed the title of guest because I had come the farthest. But did my efforts help with Zumbo? They did not.

While I am crawling around mountains so high I have to fight off Dalai Lamas trying to convert me to monastic life, Zumbo walks up to the crest of the first little hill. There he spies an elk about ten mile away.

Quick as a wink, and I have a pretty quick wink, he whips out his trusty elk call and gives a blast. The bull elk raises his head, gets a fix on Zumbo's position, and races across several mountain ranges and two major rivers to get to him. When the elk is at 18 feet, Zumbo draws his bow and fires.

It would please me greatly at this point to say that he missed. But my luck had been running badly all day, and he drilled the elk with a near-perfect shot.

The elk charged away madly for about 50 yards, then folded up dead in mid-gallop and rolled another 30 yards onto a logging road. I can't tell you how disgusted I was. And by the time the hunt was over, my having had not a shot, I was more disgusted than ever.

So I just wanted to tell you the real truth. And now that you have read this, if you want to put this book back on the rack it is okay with me. By the way, I expect to write a book on elk hunting before long, but I don't think I will have Zumbo write the foreword.

Clare Conley
Editor-in-Chief
Outdoor Life

Introduction

This book has been a labor of love. While a certain amount of paper research was required, most of the research took place in the sweet mountain air of America's West with an elk tag in my pocket and Bertha slung over my shoulder.

For 20 years I have wanted to write a book on elk hunting, and I knew I'd have to practice what I preached before attempting a project of this magnitude. I had to get out and hunt elk every way I could and learn as much as possible to pass those experiences on in a book.

And I did. Since 1978, when I gave up a comfortable government job and became a full-time outdoor writer, I hunted elk in at least three states each year, sometimes four and five. I hunted with 60 pounds on my back, from atop my wonderful half-Arab horse, Silver, with my 4WD vehicles, and with a number of outfitters in every top elk state. I made lots of mistakes and learned the hard way that elk hunting is the toughest, most unpredictable big game pursuit in the country.

While climbing that long, uphill road to be an experienced elk hunter with enough savvy to write a book, I met many fantastic people who helped me along. Like Jack Atcheson Sr., for example, a hunter's consultant, booking agent, taxidermist, outfitter, and one of the most skilled elk hunters I know. Jack took me on my first Montana elk hunt and arranged several hunts around the West for me afterward. And Billy Stockton, a Montana outfitter I call Mountain Boss, who taught me a great deal about elk, and whom I respect for all his talents, particularly in the woods. And the dozens of outfitters and guides in Montana, Wyoming, Colorado, Idaho, Utah, and New Mexico who instructed me about horses and packing and bugling and just about everything I know about elk hunting.

I hope you'll learn a little something about elk from this book. I've tried to describe every technique possible to hunt those wonderful animals, as well as the different environments they live in. There's also information on planning your own elk hunt, hiring an outfitter, which state or province to hunt in, handling horses, getting your meat out, bowhunting, muzzleloading, elk guns and optics, and just about every subject I thought should be covered to make this a comprehensive and helpful book.

Once you read this book I'm sure you'll see that I truly love elk, and I love being in elk woods, listening to their wild, maddening screams, or stillhunting them in a thick forest, or tracking them in the snow, or whatever it takes to seek them successfully.

I'll wager that you'll feel just as I do when you hunt elk. The big animals are magnificent, charismatic creatures that have no equal. I give never-ending thanks to the Almighty for letting me enjoy these noble animals, and I'm also grateful that far-sighted people had the good sense to protect our dwindling elk herds around the turn of the century when the big animals were almost driven to extinction.

Enjoy this book, as I'm sure you'll enjoy elk and elk hunting.

Jim Zumbo
Cody, Wyoming

CHAPTER 1

All About Elk

Before the turn of the century, the scream of a bull elk almost vanished into oblivion. If it were not for protected herds in national parks and other sanctuaries, elk may have become extinct. Tragically, one elk subspecies indeed was driven to extinction, and another is thought to be extinct as well.

Ernest Thompson Seton, a famous American naturalist, estimated that there were 10 million elk in North America when our country was settled by Europeans. Because of excessive hunting and reduction of habitat, less than 100,000 elk remained by 1910. Populations continued to decline, until 90,000 or so were left by 1920. Of that total, almost half lived in Yellowstone Park, Teton National Forest, and western Canada. In other regions, small herds occupied isolated mountain areas inaccessible to humans.

Before 1900, elk were managed with little or no regard to their future. Bag limits were nonexistent or totally lacking. Besides being sought for food, elk were eliminated by stockmen because elk compete with livestock for forage.

As elk populations plummeted, it became obvious to

Elk herds were seriously depleted around the turn of the century, and sights such as this were rare. Only a few areas in the West had elk populations.

conservationists that something had to be done. In 1909, elk were fed near Jackson Hole, Wyoming, to sustain them during the critical winter months and to lure them away from croplands. Feeding continued through the years, and the area was set aside as the National Elk Refuge. Today, some 10,000 elk are fed annually on the refuge.

The second decade of the 2Oth century was critical to the future of North American elk. During that period, western states initiated transplant programs to build elk herds. Here are some examples:

Arizona. In 1913, 86 elk were stocked in the Sitgreaves National Forest. At that time, elk were completely extinct in Arizona. As a result of that transplant and others afterward, Arizona's elk herds are now thriving.

Colorado. There were an estimated 500 elk in 1910.

These elk winter each year at the National Elk Refuge in Jackson Hole, Wyoming. The refuge served as a core for transplanting elk to other states in the early 1900's. About 10,000 elk migrate to the refuge annually.

From 1912 to 1928, 350 elk from Jackson Hole were stocked during 14 transplant projects. The results were dramatic and are responsible for Colorado's status as having more elk than any other state.

Idaho. Elk numbered less than 1,000 in 1918. As a result of 675 animals obtained from Yellowstone Park and Jackson Hole, herds were successfully established. Idaho is now a top elk state, with an annual harvest of about 10,000 animals.

New Mexico. By 1910, every elk here had been killed. Between 1911 and 1914, some 60 elk were obtained from Yellowstone Park and released in the state. The stocking was successful; now there are more than 12,000 elk in New Mexico.

And so it went in practically every western state. Trans-

Winter takes its toll everywhere even on the National Elk Refuge where animals are fed daily.

This is a fine mature bull, certainly the epitome of the elk in America and the type elk that states are striving for in quality management programs.

Prescribed burning is a common management tool that improves elk habitat. This photo illustrates the results of fire management in an aspen patch. Note the succulent regrowth. Elk were seen feeding in this vegetation before the photo was taken.

planted animals, mostly from Yellowstone Park and Jackson Hole, were the basis for many elk herds in western mountain ranges. Total protection of those newly established herds allowed them to thrive and reproduce. As populations increased, wildlife officials began transplanting elk within their states to vacant habitats. Today, elk occupy much of their historic range, with about 750,000 elk alive and well in the West.

When settlers first came to America, six subspecies of elk lived in our forests and on our prairies.

The Eastern elk, *Cervus elaphus canadensis*, dwelled in the eastern half of America and eastern Canada and is now thought to be extinct.

The Manitoban elk, *Cervus elaphus manitobensis*, occupied several central states and central Canadian provinces.

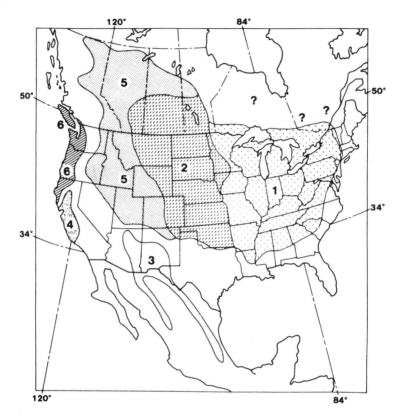

Original distribution of 1. Eastern elk, 2. Manitoban elk, 3. Merriam elk, 4. Tule elk, 5. Rocky Mountain elk, and 6. Roosevelt elk, based on available records

They currently number about 10,000, most of them residing in Riding Mountain National Park, Prince Albert National Park, and Duck Mountain Provincial Park—all in Canada.

The Rocky Mountain elk, *Cervus elaphus nelsoni*, lives in the Rockies and currently inhabits most of its historic range. Small herds have been established in some eastern and midwestern states. This is the most popular elk subspecies among hunters, numbering about 600,000.

The Roosevelt's elk, *Cervus elaphus roosevelti*, lives in the western coastal forests from California to Alaska. This ani-

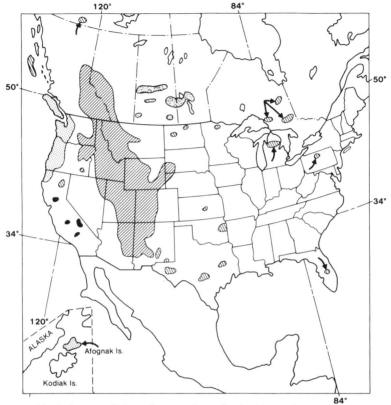

Distribution of elk in North America as of 1978, based on the compilation of information provided by provincial and state wildlife agencies (map courtesy of the Wildlife Management Institute).

mal, also known as the Olympic elk, numbers about 90,000.

The Tule elk, *Cervus elaphus nannodes*, has a population of about 1,000 in eight California counties. It is not hunted.

The Merriam elk, *Cervus elaphus merriami*, occupied Mexico and parts of New Mexico and Arizona. It is now extinct; the last of its kind was killed around 1905.

For size comparisons, the Merriam elk was thought to

be the largest of all the subspecies. The Roosevelt's elk is the largest of the existing subspecies, followed by the Manitoban, then the Rocky Mountain, and finally the Tule.

The Rocky Mountain elk has the largest antlers; the Tule has the smallest. Roosevelt's elk often have a "crown" at the tops of their antlers. Two or three tines grow closely together, giving a webbed appearance.

A pair of antlers from a mature Rocky Mountain elk will weigh between 20 and 30 pounds. As calves, bulls have no antlers. As yearlings (1½ years old) they normally have spikes that are generally from 14 to 20 inches in length. When they attain the age of 2½, they usually have four or five tines on each antler, and are commonly called "brush bulls" or "rag horns." Bulls that are 3½ years old and older develop more mass and longer antlers, and typically grow five or six tines on each side. Elk that reach the age of 4½ years and older commonly have a typical six-point configuration. Bulls with seven points to the side are much sought after by hunters but are uncommon. In some circles, a "royal bull" is a seven-pointer, but contemporary hunters and writers usually classify a six-point bull as a royal, and a seven-pointer as an imperial bull. This point is commonly debated around campfires and will probably never be settled for once and for all.

The size and number of points on a bull's antlers are dependent on a number of factors, including age, nutrition, and genetics. Gary J. Wolfe, ranch manager for the famed Vermejo Park in New Mexico, made an intensive study to determine the relationship between age and antler development. Wolfe examined 480 bulls and found that antler size increased each year until 10½ years of age, then decreased in size thereafter. The number of antler points reached a maximum at 7½ years of age and remained generally stable afterward. Ninety percent of the six-point bulls were at least 4½ years old, and all of the bulls scoring at least 300 Boone and Crockett points were 4½ years old or older. The best trophy-class bulls were between 7½ and 10½ years old.

Elk weights vary widely, but mature bulls generally

An elk's antlers grow at an incredible rate. This Wyoming bull was photographed on July 4th, and in just six weeks his antlers will be fully grown.

Besides providing sport for hunters, elk offer recreational values to people who enjoy watching and photographing them.

weigh between 700 and 1,000 pounds live weight. Cows are smaller in stature than bulls of the same age.

The name *elk* has been confusing over the years on an international basis. In Europe, moose are called elk, and Europeans often refer to our elk as wapiti. Though there is some disagreement among wildlife biologists and taxonomists, the elk of North America is so closely related to the Eurasian red deer that both are the same genus and species.

Our beloved elk is a favorite quarry among big game hunters around the world. Because of this interest, western states are managing elk to meet the recreational demand. As this book is written, elk populations are flourishing in much of the West.

Although the hunter's typical impression of an elk is a big, mature bull, most of the harvest actually consists of yearling and 2½-year-old bulls, and cows and calves. In many areas, elk simply do not live long enough to grow large antlers. Obviously, the biggest elk live in backcountry regions or in areas where they're undisturbed or hunting is restricted.

In order to offer quality hunting, most states have special units set aside where tags are limited and available through a lottery. As an example, Colorado has recently established 20 quality units that offer hunters a good chance of seeing a mature bull. Because of an unlimited permit system in Colorado, the bull-to-cow ratio is poor, with three bulls per 100 elk in some areas. Spike bulls make up the largest percentage of the harvest, with less than 10 percent of the kill in many areas consisting of six-point bulls. The quality-hunt program will bring superb elk hunting back to Colorado, as well as other states that have similar statistics.

The future of elk hunting is bright, but there will be herd reductions in areas because winter range is quickly being destroyed to make way for urban development. Furthermore, competition between elk and livestock has, and

The backcountry horseback hunt is a fantasy of millions of American sportsmen. It is a superb outdoor experience, whether an elk is taken or not.

Winter is a time for animals to conserve energy and utilize whatever forage is available. Big game animals such as this buck mule deer and bull elk coexist on limited winter ranges.

always will be, a thorn in the elk management picture.

Given the nature of western mountains, elk must leave their high-country domains before heavy snow blankets the high elevations. Annual migrations are the answer, but elk don't stop at fences. They consume anything palatable, including hay, crops, and other valued agricultural products. As a consequence, they become liabilities in the winter, and their herds must be carefully regulated to insure harmony with the land.

There are some very positive elk management programs in the West. Idaho, for example, is currently experiencing a dramatic elk population increase after a serious decline. The great 1910 Idaho fire, which burned an enormous chunk of real estate, created perfect conditions for elk. Animals flourished in the aftermath of the burn because thickly timbered stands were consumed, and succulent vegetation sprang up in the ashes. But the nutritious forage was overgrown by

Elk behavior is a fascinating subject, and is studied intensely by modern biologists. Because of their efforts, we're learning a great deal about elk and how to manage them more effectively.

This bull paws away snow to get at grass underneath. Though elk eat browse, their chief food preference is grass throughout much of the year.

trees as the years passed, and elk no longer had a plentiful food supply. Over the last few years, more conservative hunting regulations combined with fire management programs are allowing Idaho's elk to make a fine recovery.

As another example, elk herds in Utah are making rapid gains because wildlife officials have recently taken a positive approach to elk management. For years, Utah biologists were enamored with mule deer and considered elk a bonus species. Little management was directed to elk herds. At the same time, the U.S. Forest Service commonly favored livestock over elk on public forests where there was competition between the two for forage. Happily, that philosophy has changed, and elk are being transplanted within Utah to establish new herds and bolster others. A decrease in cow and antlerless permits is allowing the herds to increase as well.

The Utah story has been echoed in other states, and herds are stable to increasing in all of them. No states report significant elk population decreases.

There is some pessimism on the horizon. As we continue to open up forests for mining, oil drilling, and logging, increased access and development will eliminate escape cover required by elk. As habitat is penetrated by new access roads, many elk will be driven into the backcountry. Those herds that tolerate man's presence will be subjected to consistent hunting pressure, precluding bulls from attaining enough maturity to develop large antlers. Nonetheless, the old saying, "Any elk is a good elk," will hold true, and most hunters will accept an antlerless animal or yearling bull.

Despite the negative aspects, elk are here to stay, and will continue to be managed as a high-priority species. And rightly so. Interest in hunting and viewing them has never been greater.

There were about 500,000 elk in North America in 1970. Now, little more than a dozen years later, there are approximately 700,000. Will elk populations ever reach one million? I fervently hope so, and I'm betting you do too.

CHAPTER 2

Scouting and Hunting Techniques

Elk country is diverse. It's also huge. Hunting techniques vary enormously and depend on a number of factors. In Colorado, for example, you might pursue elk in quaking aspen forests; in Arizona, in pinyon forests; in the northern Rockies, in thickly timbered evergreen forests; and along the West Coast, in rain forests.

This chapter will address techniques for various elk environments, as well as scouting and hunting strategies that apply everywhere.

SCOUTING

When you look for elk, remember one very basic factor: You're essentially looking for a band of animals in a vast chunk of land, usually mountainous, and usually heavily timbered. Elk aren't like deer in that they're scattered around the forest. There will be lone elk or small groups, but most will be in herds.

There's no substitute for getting among the trees and looking for elk where elk live. You can glass from a vehicle until the cows come home, but you might not be looking where you should. The elk could be on the other side of the ridge or down inside a canyon. If you don't put plenty of ground under your feet, you'll be blissfully ignorant.

Do your scouting when elk are active. That means early in the morning and late in the afternoon. If you spot a feeding herd, back off and leave them alone, unless hunting season is open and you have enough light to move in on them.

If you're scouting before the season, and you should be, don't be smug and confident if you've spotted elk. Other people might have seen them too. For that reason, try to locate as many herds as you can.

Elk are big, and they leave big tracks. If you find fresh tracks, try to figure out what the elk were doing when they made them. Were they moving from feeding to bedding areas or vice versa? Since they prefer to feed where grass is plentiful, they might be using meadows. Don't overlook small meadows deep in the forest. Elk will feed wherever they can find adequate food. When hunting pressure is heavy, they often refuse to leave the timber until dark, or not at all. Many western forests have good elk feed among the trees.

The basic ingredient of successful scouting is simply to locate fresh sign. Unlike whitetail hunting where you can watch a well-used trail or a scrape, or mule deer hunting where deer inhabit the same general areas, elk have no set patterns. They move a great deal, even when they are not hunted. Be satisfied when you find areas that show recent elk activity, and concentrate your efforts there. And when elk season opens and animals are disturbed, you need to start from square one. They're unpredictable and can go anywhere, perhaps miles away to a completely new area where hunting pressure is absent or minimized.

Don't be too ambitious when you scout. If you run into bedded elk, you could spook them into the next county. If you have an idea elk are bedding in a patch of timber because of sign leading into it, don't disturb it until you have a

These aspens were "barked" by elk, which means animals ate bites of bark. This sign doesn't tell the hunter much except that elk were in the area at one time. Don't rely on this kind of sign while hunting.

rifle in your hands, a tag in your pocket, and the season is open.

If you spot a herd feeding but can't see any bulls, don't let your curiosity get the best of you, because you could kick the herd out of the area if you get too close or the wind betrays you.

Like other big game animals, elk leave signs besides footprints. They rub trees with their antlers in early fall to shed the velvet coating, and they rub trees and rip bushes and saplings apart when they're in the rut. If you're hunting after the rut and see slashed and "barked" trees, that doesn't mean elk will be in the area. But it does mean that bulls were there in the recent past, and there's every reason to believe they'll frequent the place afterward. If elk are at-

This is the kind of sign to look for. Outfitter Bruce Scott points to a fresh rub made by an elk in Idaho's Selway Wilderness. The top of the rub was 8 feet off the ground.

tracted to an area, that means they like it. If they like it, they might be close by.

Wallows are also good places to find bulls. More details on wallows follow in this chapter.

Scouting shouldn't be intense, unless you're a trophy hunter and want to see bulls as close as possible. Only then should you press the animals at the risk of spooking them.

STILLHUNTING

This is the toughest hunting technique, because it's done on the elk's turf—in the woods that are usually dense and noisy. The term infers that the hunter remains still, but that's not how it's interpreted by the hunting fraternity. Stillhunting means moving, ever so slowly. It means watching and listening, and in elk hunting it also means smelling.

Elk aren't extremely difficult to sneak up on when they're bedded. I'm not suggesting that they're not wary; they just aren't as tuned to the forest as other animals are. I believe this is so because elk are noisy. If you observe a herd of bedded elk, you'll invariably see one or two animals on their feet, nibbling around, and lazily moving about. As they walk, their legs snap small twigs and break branches. This is part of the elk's world. They're used to such sounds.

As you slip around, you might break branches, and chances are good that you can get fairly close to the herd. But don't count on it working all the time. I've been caught red-handed many times by alert elk that heard me trying to sneak up on them.

Of course, if you break big branches with fervor and sound like an elephant storming through the forest, no elk will stand for that. I'm talking about the occasional branch that you might break as you slip along.

I probably will say it 20 times in this book: The wind will be your worst enemy. Elk have superb noses and will scent you long before you know they're in the area. Always move with the breeze in your face, never at your back. And don't be fooled into thinking that there are calm days when the wind isn't blowing. Those days are virtually nonexistent. A small feather tied with thread to a button on your jacket will show you which way the air is wafting about.

If you smell elk, ease your rifle to your shoulder and be prepared to see or hear something. Elk have a distinct pungent odor and can be easily detected by even inexperienced hunters. It's possible to smell them 100 yards or more away.

Elk will occasionally allow you to walk by while they stay bedded, knowing full well who and what you are. I once spotted an elk lying down and walked to within 20 yards to see if it had horns. We played a staring game with each other until it bounced up from under the tree and leaped into a thicket. The joke was on me. I never got a shot, and I was amazed at the nerves of the elk, which turned out to be a very good bull.

When prowling about the forest, don't look for a big animal. Look for a patch of yellow, brown, or cream-colored fur. Elk blend in well with the woods, particularly since they seek thick places to bed down.

Stillhunting will test your skills, and you'll need to have a strong body as well as a savvy brain. Don't be surprised if you walk and climb more than on any other hunt in your life.

DRIVING

Elk are tough to drive because they live in big country and it's hard to figure where they'll run. It's also hard to decipher where they'll be in order to drive them. Furthermore, elk are stubborn and may refuse to leave cover, preferring instead to mill about in the timber.

A few years ago, while hunting with outfitter Keith Rush of Butte, Montana, I was sitting adjacent to a patch of timber while Keith and his guides were trying to stir up elk and boot them out where I could see them. A horse accident a couple days before incapacitated me a bit and I couldn't

These hunters are about to divide up to make a drive. Elk drives aren't very predictable, but they work at times, especially when plenty of hunters are involved.

walk much. We knew elk were in the timber because we rode around the perimeter on horseback and saw where elk had gone in but hadn't come out. Tracks in the snow easily marked their movements.

The elk didn't come out but stayed in the cover. The drivers caught glimpses of them in the trees, but the animals wouldn't cooperate.

On another hunt recently, an elk drive worked well, and wouldn't have worked at all if it wasn't for the guide's ingenuity. I was hunting with outfitter Dave Lloyd of Teton Country Outfitters in the famed Gros Ventre area of western Wyoming. Jim Lloyd, Dave's son, placed several of us around a big stand of timber while he and other guides made a drive through it. Before leaving, Jim picketed three horses at key spots around the forest. The horses were tied in areas that we couldn't watch; Jim figured any spooked

This nice bull was the result of a well-designed drive.

elk would see the horses, run back into the timber, and dash out near a hunter. The plan worked slicker than January ice. A bull and two cows were about to evict the cover when they spotted a picketed horse and changed directions. A moment later, one of the hunters killed the bull as it raced out of the trees.

Driven elk are apt to do most anything. If a behavior pattern exists, I'd say that spooked elk prefer to run uphill and generally will top a ridge in a low saddle.

Elk are also known to behave like whitetails and exit driven cover by running in fingers of timber or brush rather than exposing themselves. I'm speaking of spooked elk here and not terrified elk. The latter will run across Main Street to escape hunters and never think twice about doing so. Terrified elk are those that have been thoroughly scared by plenty of hunters and probably shot at any number of times.

Driving elk is unpredictable, but it often has happy results. About all you can do is try it and see.

TRACKING

Because elk are large animals, tracking them might appear to be a simple task. It stands to reason that large animals make large tracks. While elk are easier to track than deer, that doesn't mean you can find the critters that made the tracks.

An immediate requirement in tracking is to first identify the animal that made the prints. A big bull track is readily obvious, but there are some big cows that could confuse you. Some hunters figure they can tell bull from cow tracks, but I haven't found a technique that's foolproof. There are, however, some general guidelines.

If the animal detours around a narrow spot in a trail, it's likely to be a bull since its antlers might not have squeezed between the trees.

In the event that you locate a place where the animal urinated, try to determine the position of the body. If the

Bugling is the highest-touted elk technique, but actually less than 10 percent of America's elk hunters are afield during the rut. Most seasons start after the rut.

urine is under the midsection of the animal, you're tracking a bull. If the urine is behind the animal, a cow made the track. Also, bulls squirt when they urinate; cows puddle.

If you're following a single large track, it's probably a bull. Cows don't travel alone much. A large track and a small one were probably made by a cow and calf.

Tracks in cattle country may be misleading if you can't differentiate between elk and cattle prints. Basically, cattle have rounded toes, and elk have pointed toes. If you're still confused, look for droppings. Elk void pellets; cattle leave pie-shaped excretion.

The time of year is a big factor in figuring how to catch up to an elk. If you're trailing a bull during the breeding season, prepare for a long hike. Elk are restless then and wander about almost aimlessly, looking for cows. They don't eat or sleep much and can cover miles in a single night.

After the rut, elk do a lot of hiding and don't move

much, especially when hunters are present. If you pick up a fresh track, you can usually catch up to the animal in heavy cover.

During the late season, heavy snow triggers the annual migration from the upper elevations to winter ranges. If you cut tracks, you might have a long journey to find the elk. They could travel a dozen miles or more in a few hours to get to their winter feeding areas.

When you track, always figure the quarry will be bedded in dense cover. For some reason, I've found that elk prefer to bed in evergreens. One of my favorite hunting areas is on a series of ridges blanketed with quaking aspens. Stands of Douglas fir trees grow on the western points of the ridges, and I can almost wager that elk will feed in and around the aspens by night and bed in the firs by day.

The best time to track elk is in the morning, as soon as you can see. If you can cut fresh tracks, you might locate the animals as they're moving. It might also be possible to circle and ambush them from ahead if you have an idea where they're going. It doesn't make much sense to start tracking elk in the late afternoon. Any tracks you find will probably have been made early that morning, and the elk will have been bedded all day. They'll be ready to leave their beds and start feeding, so it's often wise to find a vantage point and wait for them to reverse their pattern and come back out to feed as the sun lowers.

If you're tracking in aspens or in cover where visibility is good, don't waste time moving too slowly if elk are already bedded. They'll likely be long gone from the aspens and will be in heavier cover. As you approach densely vegetated areas, assume the elk are in every one of them. If you're reasonably sure that elk are in a particular patch of timber but want to be positive, back off from the track and make a big circle around the suspected area. If no tracks lead out, you're on third base headed for home plate, but don't figure you're about to score a run until you tie your tag to the elk. Determine the wind direction, and move in

Bull elk wallow just before or during the rut. If you find a fresh wallow, watch it closely. It might produce a good bull. (Photo by Kathy Etling).

from the downwind side. If possible, choose an elevated route so you can see into the cover more easily.

Fresh tracks are exciting and build confidence. You know elk were recently in the area, and you might figure all you have to do is follow long enough and the elk is yours. Don't be too confident. You might catch up to the elk without too much problem, but the tough part is seeing the animal first or hitting it as it flushes. Don't let a smoking track push you too fast. Play it slow and easy, because somewhere at the end of the track, a living, breathing elk is existing, and it will do everything in its power to escape. You'd better be good to make it yours.

STALKING

I define stalking as spotting an elk and then sneaking up to it for a shot. This is seldom easy, because time is

Stalking is an effective way of hunting elk. Feeding animals are located early in the morning and late in the afternoon and carefully stalked.

always your biggest enemy. If you see elk in the morning, you won't have much time to move to within shooting range before they drift out of the open and into thick timber. If you see them in late afternoon, you'll be fighting darkness to get in close enough.

In areas where elk are undisturbed, they often come out to feed early enough to give you plenty of time to move. That was the situation I encountered on a recent hunt I took with outfitter Ken Smith of Orofino, Idaho.

We were deep in the Selway Wilderness, so deep that it required a bush plane ride to reach a wilderness airstrip. From there, a 15-mile horseback ride got us to camp, and each day we rode horseback for a dozen miles to reach the hunting area.

The daily strategy was to ride out of camp at about 8

Horses are a fact of life in elk country. Most outfitters and serious elk hunters use horses extensively.

a.m. each day and start looking for elk around 1:00 in the afternoon. Without fail, we'd spot elk dribbling out of the timber to feed between 2:00 and 3:00. With binoculars and spotting scope, we looked the elk over carefully, searching for a good bull. When one was spotted, we'd make a stalk, which was often a mile or more.

The hunt ended on a wonderful note. We spotted a big bull just before dark one day, and the next afternoon we made a stalk and located him. We blundered into several small herds of cows and calves on the way, but luckily, they didn't spook the bull. I killed him after a two-hour stalk. He was a beauty, with massive antlers having seven points on one side and six on the other.

When stalking elk, use screening cover as much as possible, no matter how far away the quarry is. Plan the attack so the wind is in your favor, and don't try to get too close. As always, hidden cows in the area could betray your presence.

Before hunting, it's always a good idea to figure a strategy with companions. Several people hunting according to a plan are often more effective than hunters wandering around on their own.

STAND HUNTING AND HUNTING THE WALLOW

This technique probably accounts for fewer elk harvested than any other strategy. It involves waiting for elk to show up on a trail or near a waterhole, meadow, or wallow.

Though elk use trails, their movement patterns aren't consistent enough to warrant spending much time watching trails. Exceptions are paths used by elk to get to feeding, bedding, or wallowing spots, but if you're going to watch an area, it's often a better idea to watch the place where you expect elk to show rather than trails. This kind of hunting has a good chance of success if elk are undisturbed and are using the same behavior habits every day. If so, you might very well set up an ambush.

Locate your stand in an elevated vantage point, if possible, because you'll likely be in timber or brush. When selecting a spot, consider the prevailing wind direction and degree of visibility from the stand. Break off critical branches that obscure your view.

When stand hunting, be prepared to get to the spot before daylight, and figure on leaving it after shooting hours are over. This means you must travel in the dark both ways. Make sure you can find the stand in the night, and likewise be sure you can find your way to your vehicle, camp, horse, or road in the dark.

If you know elk are feeding regularly in a meadow every afternoon, locate your stand so you can make a shot from it. Keep movement to a minimum. Elk are nervous when they're in the open and it's still light.

Elk water at various times, but often they will visit a waterhole just before feeding in late afternoon. Plan your strategy accordingly.

Wallows are mudholes that bull elk dearly love to roll around in. If you've hunted elk enough, you've no doubt seen bulls caked with dried mud. Biologists say the wallowing habit is caused by a bull's ardor around breeding time and is an important part of their fall ritual.

It's quite easy to determine if a mudhole is being wallowed in, because the soft earth shows clear prints. If you find an active wallow, watch it in the late afternoon. Bulls will commonly visit wallows every day.

You can find wallows almost everywhere. Small springs and seeps on mountainsides are likely places, and areas adjacent to beaver ponds and creeks are suspect as well. The best wallows look like they've been used by generations of hogs.

If you find several wallows in a small area with plenty of rubbed trees nearby, watch it and keep the place to yourself. You've found an elk playground, and it could very likely pay off handsomely. I know some hunters who kill bulls around the same wallows year after year.

Vary your strategy according to the hunt conditions. And don't give up if your efforts are fruitless. Contrary to other kinds of big game hunting, you probably won't see very many elk on your hunt. You might see only a handful, and you might see none at all. Hunt hard until the very last minute of the last day. You'll never know when the magic moment might occur. Remember, you aren't going to punch your elk tag if you sit in camp or snooze in the sun. I'm betting that elk hunting will be the toughest you've ever experienced. Keep a positive attitude, or you're licked.

CHAPTER 3

Bugling for Elk

There are many aspects of elk that set them apart from other big game animals. They're big, they're handsome, they live in America's most magnificent landscape, and they're a challenge to hunt. But there's one feature that endears them to the hearts of hunters everywhere. That's the scream of a bull during the mating season. When I hear it, goosebumps riddle my arms and the back of my neck. I've never become complacent about the sound, and I've heard it countless times. It's a wild noise, one that evokes something aboriginal, stirs something primitive and dormant inside our civilized bodies.

I'd heard an elk bugle long before I moved west in 1960. That event occurred as I watched a wildlife program on TV while living in the East. The sound mesmerized me, and it produced a restlessness, a yearning that one day had to be satisfied.

Many years passed before I heard the song of a bull elk in the wild. It happened in Yellowstone Park, in a big meadow near Norris Campground. I watched, entranced, as two bulls vented their rage and bluffed each other for the

33

precious herd of disinterested cows that fed on the frosted yellow grass.

As I watched, I recalled the hundreds of stories I'd read in magazines, written by hunting writers who pursued elk each fall by calling them with artificial whistles, luring them within rifle range. It seemed amazing to me that elk could be duped so readily, and I vowed then that I'd someday hunt them during the bugling season.

Now, after dozens of hunts, I can vividly recall the shivering excitement I felt that day in Yellowstone. That excitement was responsible for my decision to live in elk country, and I know now that life, for me, is not complete unless I can hear those wild screams every September, when the quaking aspens renounce their green foliage and transform their delicate leaves to brilliant hues of gold, yellow, and orange.

It matters not that I kill an elk each fall. Just being out there in the forest, smelling the smells, feeling the wafting breezes in my face, and hearing those marvelous animals screaming with lust and rage is enough.

It is no secret that elk hunting is at its very best during the bugling period. Practically every big game species is vulnerable during the mating season; elk are no exception. During this time, bulls are distracted by the breeding urge and behave differently than they do during any other period of the year. They're on the move constantly, feeding and sleeping little, and always seeking or guarding cows. Competition between bulls is intense, which is precisely the reason why hunting is so good during the rut.

It's no surprise that most states offer elk hunting after the rut. Wildlife officials indicate that holding the general season during the bugling period would result in the harvest of too many large elk, perhaps to the detriment of the herd.

Most states offer hunting during the rut in selected backcountry areas as well as in special quality units that require a lottery draw to obtain a tag. In Idaho, for example, you can hunt early in the vast Selway Wilderness Area; in

Hunting elk during the bugling period is the most exciting time to hunt them. Bugling itself is a great challenge and has a large following among hunters.

Montana, in the Bob Marshall Wilderness Area; in Wyoming, in backcountry areas adjacent to Yellowstone Park.

If you're a bowhunter, you can have your pick of most regions in practically every state. Bow seasons generally coincide with the rut to give archers a bit of an assist.

So far in this chapter, I've painted a rosy picture— if you hunt during the rut, your bull is assured. That's a most optimistic attitude, but in practicality it doesn't work that way. Despite a bull's susceptibility throughout the breeding season, he's not a nitwit. He's wary, he's cagey, and he's seldom a pushover.

Timing is all-important in hunting a rutting bull. The breeding season usually occurs from mid-September to early October, but it can't be counted on to take place during a

Bulls thrash the ground frequently during the rut as they vent their rage on any natural objects that are at hand.

specific date each year. It would be nice if bulls rutted as precisely as the swallows that annually return to Capistrano, but they don't.

There are all sorts of factors that attempt to explain the rut timetable, but I haven't seen any yet that are reliable. Moon phases, weather, elevational differences, and others are usually cited as integral elements. As far as I can tell, none can be depended on.

During a recent season, one outfitter friend called to tell me that bulls were absolutely crazy, screaming their brains out. At the same time, another outfitter 100 miles away said he hadn't heard an elk bugle in days. Both were first-class operators hunting prime elk country.

Storms will often affect the rut. During a recent Montana bowhunting season, outfitter Billy Stockton's clients had done remarkably well the week before our party arrived. Of six hunters, four killed elk. A snowstorm rolled in the day our hunt started and silenced the animals. For three days we hadn't heard a bull. As the weather warmed, elk resumed bugling, and we arrowed two bulls. One member of our party had opportunities at 11 different bulls that were called within bow range.

The actual bugle call of an elk is more of a fluted whistle. It starts low, ends high, and is usually followed by grunts. To me, the grunts sound more like the whine of a puppy dog in the backyard, wanting to be let into the house. The bugle sound lasts a few seconds, and various writers say it hits three, four, or five notes, depending on who you care to read and believe. My wife is a piano teacher, and her trained ear often picks up different notes from the same bull as he bugles several times.

Unlike the consistent yelp of a hen turkey or the honk of a Canada goose, an elk's bugle varies a great deal. I've heard bugling elk sound like braying jackasses. More than once I've heard terrible bugles and passed them off as being made by other hunters, only to find that real bulls were making them.

Elk will often grunt without bugling, and they'll often rip in to a grunt call without hesitation while at the same time ignoring or backing off from a bugle challenge.

It's common belief that big bulls have hoarser voices than smaller bulls. That's true to a degree, but I've been fooled plenty of times. Every now and then, a photographer buddy and I make friendly wagers on the stature of a bull by listening to him bugle. We'll hear an elk in the timber and guess how big he is. We're often surprised when an elk with a thin, reedy voice turns out to be king of the mountain, or when an elk with a hoarse, deep bugle shows up wearing modest antlers.

Spike bulls are generally easily identified. Their high-pitched short bugle readily gives them away.

Cows and calves are as vocal as bulls, though their sounds are not as apparent. They communicate by making mewing sounds. If you aren't familiar with it, you'd swear a herd of alley cats had invaded the forest.

If you haven't been elk hunting before, or if you have little experience, there are a number of ways to learn how to call. The best way is to listen to bulls in the flesh. Zoos, municipal parks, and other sanctuaries that have captive elk are good places to watch and listen. An alternative is to buy an instructional tape and practice until you can imitate a bull. I know of about a half-dozen tapes made by different experts. You can find them in mail-order catalogs for hunters or in magazine advertisements.

Don't worry about imitating an elk exactly. If anything, you should know how to interpret a bull's bugle by his actions and then reacting accordingly. More on that will follow in this chapter.

Elk bugle calls have been around a long time. I believe I own every type manufactured, and I've made my own out of garden hose, metal tubing, and plastic polyethylene pipe. I don't perceive myself to be an expert elk caller, but I've managed to bugle in several dozen bulls.

Of late, a handful of manufacturers have produced superb calls made out of plastic tubing. Some calls come with a detachable mouthpiece to allow you to grunt. Some calls are made especially for grunting and are called grunt tubes.

But the biggest innovation in the industry is the mouth diaphragm call, which is absolutely amazing once you've perfected it. I'm still trying to master the confounded things and am getting better as I keep practicing. They aren't easy to learn to use, but they're a must for every serious elk hunter. Besides the almost-perfect calls you can make with them, your hands are free to use your rifle or bow as a bull approaches.

A bull's reaction to a call depends largely on his attitude. By attitude, I mean he can be hot, luke warm, or cold.

A hot bull will dash in to anything that resembles a challenging elk. I once had an enraged elk charge me as I was riding a horse through the timber. The noise of my steed

Elk usually bluff each other during the bugle season, but frequently engage in actual battle as this pair is doing.

breaking branches and twigs set the bull off. He ran almost on top of me and flipped tin cup over teakettle when he saw me and my horse. Elk season wasn't open, so I laughed and watched him tear up the woods getting out of there. Other times I've had elk bugle and run down half a mountain to investigate me because they heard my horse's hooves on a rocky trail.

A hot bull bugles constantly, answers your calls instantly, and is apt to be all over you before you can get your gun or bow up. Practically any call will work on this boy, whether it's good or bad.

A lukewarm bull hasn't quite made his mind up about you, the caller, and you'll need to be devious and cagey to outsmart him. A lukewarm bull bugles every now and then, and may move away from you or circle you to catch your scent. You'll have to outmaneuver him to get a shot.

A cold bull will require all your talents. He'll be one of the toughest critters you've ever set after in the woods. He'll bugle very infrequently, just enough to let you know he's around, and often he won't bugle at all. You'd better know how to call and how to hunt elk in order to tag this fellow.

Bulls bugle because of various motives. Over the years, I've been fortunate to have observed elk frequently during the rut, and I've tried to reason why they carry on and react the way they do. I've spent at least 125 days in Yellowstone Park during the peaks of breeding seasons for the last dozen years, and I've learned a bit about elk behavior. That's not to say I've got them figured out. Whenever I think I do, they foil my anticipations and react differently.

I might mention that Yellowstone's bulls are wild animals. Most are never seen by tourists until the rut. At that time, normally wary bulls vacate the backcountry and consort with cows that tolerate humans. The bulls endure people because that's where the cows are, and they become visible to observers.

There are essentially three types of bulls that you'll pursue during the rut. The *herd bull* has cows and intends

This herd bull will be a tough one to draw away from his harem. A bull such as this will be reluctant to leave his cows for fear another bull might take over.

to keep them; the *serious challenger* is a mature bull who has no cows but wants them; and the *wishful thinker* is a spike bull who is either content to stay in the periphery of the herd or to run around the forest, not sure what he's looking for. Let's take them one at a time.

The herd bull is tough to call in, because he's satisfied with the girls in his harem. He isn't likely to leave them to meet a challenger, unless he's feeling particularly mean and nasty that day. I've seen herd bulls bust through timber to chase off a challenger, and I've seen others bugle with nary a care. Most, however, will move their cows away from the challenger.

If a bull answers but is either staying in one place or steadily moving off, chances are good you're working a herd bull. One option that is often successful is to press the attack and move in on him. Note the wind, and approach slowly.

Bugle every minute or so, and if he stays where he is or continues to slowly travel away, keep moving in. You might get him mad enough to make him investigate you. If he moves away, circle and try him from another angle. Again, watch the wind. The wind is more important than any bugle or grunt call you'll ever make. If you err with a call, you can generally make up for it. But if you err with the wind and the bull whiffs you, the old boy is out of your life for the time being.

Remember that a herd bull won't travel very far from his cows to look you up. Three hundred yards or so is about maximum. Get in close, as close as you dare.

If you aren't getting anywhere, try using a different call. You should carry several calls with different voice ranges. Should the bull reject one, a call that imitates a smaller bull might work. You might be intimidating him by sounding like a boss elk, and he might not want to meet up with you and lose his cows. But if you sound like a smaller bull, he might decide to charge in and kick your fanny.

When switching calls, wait several minutes and come in from a completely different position. Make him think the first challenger gave up and a smaller one entered the scene.

If the switch to a different call doesn't work, try the grunt tube. This voice often works when nothing else will.

The deadliest way to knock off a herd bull is to get between him and his cows. This usually isn't easy, but if you can do it, Katie bar the door. You might have to shoot out of self-defense.

Another tactic is to imitate a cow elk. Use the diaphragm call, and make sure you're close enough so the bull can hear you. Don't call loudly with the cow call, or it will come off unnaturally.

If an elk barks, the jig is up. A cow has winded or spotted you, and your efforts have probably been in vain. A barking cow always means a spooked or alerted cow. She'll end your hunt in a hurry.

If all else fails with the herd bull, put the calls away

and stalk him silently. If he bugles intermittently, try to figure his direction of travel and ambush him. Again, watch the wind. If he becomes silent, try to cut the herd's tracks and stalk along their trail. Listen carefully because elk are noisy when they're moving. You might be able to hear them in the timber and move in unnoticed for a shot.

The serious challenger is most unhappy with his lonely state of affairs and is ready for action. He's on the move, slashing brush, tearing up the forest floor, and profoundly upset. He's the hottest bull in the woods, but don't figure him to be a lead-pipe cinch. He didn't grow into maturity by being a fool.

Most of the bulls I've killed during the rut were loners. A couple roared straight in as soon as I made the first call. Others had to be coaxed, and some had to be hunted hard.

You can usually figure you've got a loner on your hands if he bugles frequently and moves rapidly. He may run full bore through the trees from one ridge to another, teasing you with his antics.

This giant bull thrashes a sapling with his enormous horns. Note that he has already broken the right brow tine, probably from fighting another bull or slashing a tree.

If a bull plays games but won't show, play it his way. Pick up a branch from the ground and whack it smartly against other tree branches. Draw the end of the branch hard against the bark of a tree so it makes loud scratching noises. Bugle as you do so, and keep up the racket. Don't worry about spooking the bull, unless he sees or smells you. Bulls make plenty of noise in the woods and won't be alerted unless you make metallic or unnatural sounds.

The cow mew could work wonders with this bull. With the diaphragm call in your mouth, walk rapidly away from the bull and call softly. If his ardor is aroused, and it's likely to be, he might come busting after you.

Don't try to sound like a big raunchy bull when calling the loner. He's probably been whipped by bigger bulls already, and he'll be ready to slap the devil out of a smaller bull.

If the bull approaches within range and you can see only part of him, or you know he's close, give him some whiny grunts. That's often the last straw, and may lead to his final stroll in the forest.

The wishful thinker, or spike bull, may or may not come in to your call. He'll be doing so out of curiosity, so you'll need to treat him carefully. Use a call that imitates a small bull, and blow on it sparingly.

Try the cow call on the spike if he won't respond to a bugle. He might figure it's his momma or a potential girlfriend, and waltz right out where you can get a shot.

Don't underestimate the wariness of a young bull. While it's true that he's inexperienced, he's been taught well by his mother. He can give you the slip as easily as any big bull.

As a general rule, the best time to bugle is early in the morning as soon as you can see. Try to get into the hunt area while it's still dark. You'll be able to locate bugling bulls and make your move before it's light. By doing so, you'll have a chance to set up and make your pitch at shooting light.

When bulls are at the peak of the rut, they'll often bugle

Larry Jones, a master elk caller, whistles up a bull during the September rut period.

throughout the day. I killed two of the biggest bulls of my life between 11 a.m. and noon. Both were bugling at the time and didn't hesitate to seek me out.

If hunting pressure is heavy, move as deeply into the woods as you can before attempting to bugle. Don't call near camp or from a road or well-used trail. Elk quickly learn that these areas mean danger.

Bugling elk is a very specialized technique that works only a couple weeks out of the year. It's also the most fascinating and productive way to hunt, and you owe it to yourself to try it if you like to chase elk around the West. Let me forewarn you, however: Once you start messing with lovesick bulls and listening to their wild screams, you'll never be the same. I'm sure you'll keep coming back for more.

CHAPTER 4

Transition Period—Tough Time for Hunters

Elk hunting is no fun at all during the transition period. It's all work—tough, frustrating work. The woods are silent and elk are about as interested in responding to a call as they are in riding bicycles. The hunt is doubly tough if there's no snow to track elk, and worse yet, you're apt to have plenty of competition from other hunters.

My first elk hunt was a rude awakening. Like many novice hunters, I figured all I had to do was get up early in the morning, spot a herd of elk in a meadow, and stalk close enough to shoot. If the plan didn't work, I'd try the same thing in late afternoon when elk came out of the trees to feed in forest openings.

After five futile days of hunting in the Colorado Rockies, I began to get the feeling that I was doing something wrong. I hadn't seen an elk, but there was plenty of fresh sign in the area I hunted. Twice I flushed herds in the timber, but I never saw them. I ended the hunt without using my tag, and I promised myself to find out how to hunt elk. Obviously, I didn't know how.

That hunt was almost 20 years ago. Since then I've

chased elk in every Rocky Mountain state. Though I'm still skunked on some hunts, I've come to terms with elk. I know where and how they live, and I've learned how to hunt them. Even with that information, it's still necessary to find them. Therein lies the problem.

Elk are unlike deer, antelope, moose, and other western big game animals because the major part of their diet is grass. Biologists classify elk as grazers, while most other big game animals are browsers, which means they feed on woody plants or shrubs.

This forage requirement is the reason elk are known to feed in meadows and forest openings. Grass grows best in the sunlight rather than in the shaded forest. Thick stands of grass usually carpet high-elevation meadows. So it is that elk hunting and open parks go hand in hand.

The problem, however, is the fact that elk have changed their behavior patterns over the years. They still eat grass, but they've altered their feeding periods. The chief cause of this change is increased access into elk country. Logging and energy developments have required new road systems and more human intrusions in areas that have previously been undisturbed. Elk have reacted to these changes by pulling farther back into remote and lonely places, and by hiding out as soon as daylight appears.

When hunting season approaches, elk intensify their furtive habits. They seem to know what is happening when vehicles begin grinding along forest roads, camps are set up, and people start nosing about in the backcountry. By the time opening morning arrives, elk are long gone from much of their regular domain, and those that remain are almost never seen.

But human activity doesn't necessarily spook elk out of meadows as the sun rises in the morning. By nature, elk are timber-oriented and simply don't like to be exposed in the open. I've seen elk in national parks where they're never hunted behave like wild elk that are pursued by hunters.

In some remote areas, elk might dally around a bit in

During the transition season, or period after the rut, bulls are wary and spooky. They no longer bugle, and stay in thick timber most of the day. Note how alert this bull is.

the morning and spend an extra hour or so feeding in the daylight. But those elk aren't necessarily a piece of cake when it comes to locating them.

I well remember a recent hunt with *Outdoor Life* Executive Editor Vin Sparano and his son, Matt. We packed far into the Selway Bitterroot Wilderness with outfitter Bruce Scott and had high expectations of bringing home big-racked bulls. As it turned out, the elk were there all right, but they won a game of hide and seek. I was fortunate to bag a fine six-point bull, but only after we had pursued him in a thick jungle that I never want to see again. I never saw an elk in the open on that trip, and neither did the other hunters. The animals were holed up in the timber and never showed themselves. Bruce bugled my bull in after a long horseback ride and a tedious walk through dense spruce and fir trees. We were so far from the beaten trail that I'm convinced the bull had never seen another human or heard a man-operated bugle challenge that season. Even though the rut was on, the bulls were uncooperative. I'm sure they were even harder to find later on during the transition period.

When elk are obviously absent from their usual haunts, there's only one strategy: go after them in the timber. Either that or go home with an unfired rifle and nothing else but memories.

There are all sorts of ways to hunt elk in dense forests. They include stillhunting, driving, tracking, stalking, and ambushing near waterholes and wallows.

The stillhunter has the toughest mission, because the quarry is hidden and hard to find. Unlike deer, which are usually well distributed in a given area, elk live in herds. You might hunt several square miles and never locate the herd, even though the animals are active and moving about in the area you're hunting.

The only way to pinpoint a herd is to cover plenty of ground. You don't ease along in the woods, as in whitetail hunting, but move rapidly until you find fresh sign.

When you're convinced that elk are close, slow down

Jim Zumbo with a Colorado elk he took during the transition or post-bugle period. The bull had been living in a thick stand of Douglas fir, coming out only at night to feed.

and stillhunt as intently as you ever have before. You might have to travel five or 10 miles to locate elk, and it could take several days to do it.

Because elk are bigger than deer, their signs are much more obvious. It's easy to spot a fresh track, because the weight of the animal causes a distinctive imprint, whether snow is present or not.

Once you've determined the general location of an elk herd, the next step is to figure the wind direction and stalk closely. It's not difficult to approach a bunch of bedded elk, even though many eyes and ears are constantly tuned to the woods around them. I've found that it's easier to stalk several elk than a single whitetail or mule deer buck. Perhaps elk feel more secure because of their numbers. Certainly their nervous disposition is conducive to careful stalking, because they appear to be much more at ease in their daily movements than whitetails or mulies are.

Several years ago, I was hunting elk with a buddy in Utah. From a high vantage point we spotted a cow elk in the timber. She was nibbling on grass and remained in one position for a half-hour. We decided she was part of a herd, though we could see no other elk. I had already filled my tag, so I waited on the ridgetop until my friend made a stalk. An hour passed and I was sure there were no bulls in the area until I heard a rifle shot. I walked to the spot and found my buddy dressing a fine six-point bull. He had sneaked into the middle of the herd and killed the bull at a distance of 20 yards in the dense timber. The wind was right for a stalk, and the soft pine needles allowed quiet movement.

Last year, while hunting elk in Wyoming with Teton Country Outfitters, my guide Kevin McNiven convinced me that elk could be hunted in timber by smelling them first and then making a stalk. Kevin followed his nose and always moved into the wind. Three times he accurately pinpointed elk by smelling them and sneaking close, but the timber was so thick I couldn't get a shot at the fleeing animals. Elk have a distinctive odor, and it's possible to detect their presence several hundred yards away. I'd heard of smelling elk out and hunting them, and a time or two I used my nose to get in close, but Kevin was able to pick up their scent from more than a quarter-mile away. He said it simply takes concentration, a good nose, and the constant need to work with the wind and breezes.

In some areas, elk can be driven from their timbered bedding areas, but the tactic is more often a failure than a success. Elk aren't fond of leaving the shelter of trees and more often than not will refuse to break into the open, preferring instead to slip away from drivers in the timber and remain hidden. On the other hand, I've seen elk that were spooked badly enough do some amazing stunts. Once I saw a herd of two bulls and a dozen cows dash out of the forest,

Bulls spend most of their time in the timber after the rut. They don't move much, and feed only in the night and very early in the morning and late in the afternoon.

run a mile through a sagebrush flat, and pass within 100 yards of three camp trailers that were sitting in the open. The occupants of the camps grabbed their rifles and claimed both bulls.

But most of the time, elk aren't such pushovers. Several years ago, on another hunt with Vin Sparano, we were involved in a driving tactic in Montana. Vin and I sat at strategic positions while the outfitter and guides stirred elk in the timber. The plan seemed to be a cinch but the elk didn't cooperate. Instead of bounding out into the open as we had hoped, they milled about in the trees and never showed themselves. We couldn't hunt in the timber because we had both suffered minor injuries on the hunt. He had scratched a cornea from an errant twig, and I had injured my leg during a horse spill. I'm confident that we could have bagged elk if we had been able to slip around in the trees.

Jim Zumbo looks for elk in out of the way places during transition season, such as these brushy side slopes along rugged canyons where elk aren't disturbed.

When elk drives work, it's usually the young bulls and cows and calves that show. The wise old bulls aren't about to break into the open and behave like crafty whitetails.

The finest way to hunt timber-bound elk is to call them in with a bugle. As I said in other chapters, there are a couple of problems with this technique. Elk seasons normally begin in mid-October, which is past the peak of the rutting period. Generally, the rut occurs in September and early October, which means elk won't respond to a bugle during the general hunt. Several western states have September hunts, but they're in backcountry units that require plenty of preparation, transportation, and knowledge of the country. If you hunt with a bow, you'll have no problem finding an accessible place to hunt elk. Almost every state holds the elk bow season during the peak of the rut.

Tracking an elk in the timber is an effective method, but you'll need to be prepared for a long hike in most cases. Elk often travel long distances, especially if there's enough hunter pressure to keep them moving. If snow conditions are right, you can usually catch up to an elk, but you'll need to be on your toes during the final moments of the sneak. It's easy to blunder into a bedded animal when you're not paying enough attention. Remember that elk normally bed in thick timber. When you stalk, slow down, and if the track leads into dense trees, carefully check the forest ahead.

Don't look for a big animal. A patch of brown or yellow or a slight movement might betray a resting elk. One of my favorite hunting areas in Utah has a stand of timber denser than the woods around it. More than once I've found elk bedded in that particular spot rather than in the more open trees.

Harold Ullery, a veteran Wyoming outfitter, uses an interesting tactic to sneak up on elk. He packs into the backcountry, and by the time dawn appears he is high on a ridgetop where he can see for miles. By using a spotting scope he glasses the meadows and openings, and if he spots elk he makes a careful stalk. This kind of strategy must be done in those few minutes of poor light before elk head into the timber. If elk are undisturbed, they normally bed down in the timber within a quarter-mile or so of their feeding area. By seeing them leave the opening, you can determine which general area they'll be laying up in for the day.

If you try hunting elk in the timber, you must make every effort to keep unnatural noise to a minimum. Wear clothing that doesn't scrape noisily in the brush. Wool is a good choice. Stay away from cheap hunter orange hunting vests or shirts. Heavy, cumbersome boots often prevent quiet walking. Wear boots that will allow you to place your feet carefully between branches and twigs.

Remember the basic axiom in elk hunting. Animals are active when light is poor or during the night. If you aren't leaving camp in the dark, you're missing the prime time to catch elk when they're active. Chances are good that you won't see them no matter what you do, so figure on out-smarting them in the timber. That's where they live, and that's where you must hunt them. There's usually no other choice if you're hunting them during the transition time.

CHAPTER 5

Hunting Late-Season Elk

Heavily falling snowflakes obscured my view as I tried to glass the big basin below me. I hunched lower into my woolen jacket, trying unsuccessfully to escape the wet snow accumulating under my collar. It was bitterly cold; the air temperature was about 5 degrees. I wiggled my toes constantly in my heavy insulated boots, and flexed my fingers in my gloves. With a little luck, all the pain and suffering would be worth it.

I was hunting elk late in November, hoping to waylay a bull migrating out of the Montana high country. I counted on the heavy snowfall to force elk out of the upper elevations and down into their traditional winter ranges. This was the third significant snowfall of the year. About 20 inches had accumulated where I stood, and I knew it was much deeper in the higher country. I was confident that the elk would be moving.

After two hours of waiting and glassing with no results, I walked along the mountain slope, gradually working my way higher. If I could cut a fresh trail, I might be able to track elk and locate them before nightfall. It was tough

Elk migrating to winter range. The late hunt is a fine time to pursue elk, provided enough snow is available to drive them to low elevations.

going in the deep snow. I wished I could use my snowshoes, but I knew they'd be useless in the steep, rocky terrain.

Pockets of timber grew along the mountainside, and numerous deep draws sliced into the landscape. It would be easy for elk to hide in the rugged terrain.

I trudged along for an hour and finally reached the ridgetop. Plenty of mule deer tracks were evident in the snow, but there was no sign of elk.

Two hours later I struck elk tracks. A small herd of animals had slowly worked their way off the mountain, feeding as they traveled. Their meandering trails showed that they were in no hurry as they pawed through the snow and nibbled on grass beneath. I figured the elk were just a few hours ahead of me. The snow had quit earlier, but the tracks were fairly distinct, especially where the elk had moved into the cover of timber.

This is famous Deckard Flat on the Gallatin National Forest outside Yellowstone Park in Montana. Note the elk tracks. They were made by more than 1,000 elk that migrated outside the park to winter ranges.

But I had a big problem. Only two hours of light remained, and it would take me at least that long to walk out to my truck. If I continued after the elk, I'd have to make my way out in the dark. I wasn't prepared to overnight in the outdoors, although my daypack held all the survival gear I would have needed. If a new storm struck that evening I'd have difficulty getting out, and my truck would be snowed in as well.

A freshening breeze and more falling snow helped me make my decision. I'd leave the elk and try for them in the morning. That option gave me an important advantage. If I kept going now, I might blunder into the elk because of the fading light and spook them. By leaving them undisturbed, I'd have a good chance of ambushing them in the morning. I had a hunch that they wouldn't be moving fast, and I had an idea where they were.

The next morning didn't offer much improvement in the weather. It had snowed slightly during the night, but ominous clouds portended more storms. I hurried into the whiteness, hoping the elk hadn't moved much.

The sun was barely up when I topped the last ridge, I looked down and immediately saw about two dozen elk a half-mile away. They were on a windswept sidehill just adjacent to a finger of timber, feeding on the cured grass that thrust above the light covering of snow. There were three bulls in the herd of cows and calves. One bull was a decent five-point; the others were modest four-pointers.

I planned a route that would take me to the elk unseen,

Jim Zumbo with Don Laubach and Don's son, Kirk, with a bull taken on the last day of Montana's elk season just outside Yellowstone Park. The bull was leaving the snowy Park for winter range on the Gallatin Forest.

and took care not to skyline myself on the ridge. I backed off and sneaked down across a rock outcrop. If I could get into the finger of timber, I'd have a good chance of stalking to within 150 yards of the elk. The wind was in my favor, and I was counting on it to stay that way.

The stalk came off perfectly. I slipped through the firs and spruces and crawled the last few yards in the snow. I looked out at the edge of the trees and saw the elk, right where they'd been when I started the sneak.

I eased my Winchester .30/06 up into the crotch of a tree in front of me, centered the biggest bull, and sent the 165-grain Nosler bullet on its way. At the shot the bull stumbled, got back up on his feet, and burst ahead 15 yards. He stood there weaving, and I knew he'd go down permanently, but I worked another cartridge into the chamber and hit him again. This time he collapsed into the snow for good.

I walked up to him and looked him over. He was fat and in good shape. His antlers weren't huge but were good enough for me. I tagged him, rolled up my sleeves, and positioned him for field-dressing. When that chore was done, I headed out to bring back a pair of horses to pack out the meat.

Late-season elk hunting isn't always so rewarding. I've trudged more miles than I care to remember, and I've ridden plenty of horseback miles with nothing to show for my efforts. But it's a satisfying time to hunt because your chances of seeing elk are excellent. You need to follow a different set of rules, though, and you'll know you've been on a hunt when you're done. Snow and cold are always factors you need to deal with, but occasionally there are times when you can make a late hunt on bare ground.

Weather is usually the critical factor during late season. Unless serious snowstorms evict elk from their lofty domains, elk hunting can be an exercise in futility. Then too, elk are unsettled this time of year. They can be in one place on a given day, and the next day be 10 miles away.

Although elk are big, hardy creatures, they cannot sur-

Mary Lineback of Billings, Montana, with a fine bull she took
during the special late season on the Gardiner Unit near Yellowstone Park. These late hunts last 2 or 4 days. Hunt periods are
selected by a computer.

vive when winter storms pile snow deep in the upper elevations. When that happens, elk travel to winter ranges, often following the same familiar trails that they use year after year. I've been told that elk will follow the same precise routes. They step over the same branches and walk across the same rocks.

If the late-season hunter knew where those migration trails were, and if he or she was positioned at precisely the right place at the right time, the hunt would be a piece of cake. Unfortunately, that set of conditions is a rarity, though there are places where you are almost assured an elk if you can draw a tag and the snow is right. I'm referring to extra-late seasons around Yellowstone Park—during December, January, and February, when Montana issues special late permits to harvest elk migrating out of Yellowstone. There are a few very late elk hunts in other states as well.

But most late hunts are during the transition period. During this time, elk are making up their minds about moving out of summer quarters and into the winter areas, where they'll remain until the spring sunshine coaxes them back to the pine and spruce forests where the air is thin and sweet.

Hunters who try late seasons for elk have one common need: snow. If there's a time when avid hunters pray fervently, it's to ask the Almighty for plenty of white flakes to boot elk out of the high country.

In some areas, local hunters calmly go about their business, keeping an eye peeled for snowy weather. When it comes, they wait until elk make their move. Then the hunter grabs a rifle, a few cartridges, and heads for a back road where he pops a big bull elk from the tailgate of his pickup truck.

Most of us, however, are not privy to that kind of information or flexible schedule. We need to expend some time and calories to locate elk.

There are ways to help the odds, however. Elk migrations are no big secret in many areas. Practically any local who knows anything about hunting can tell you where mi-

Jim Zumbo with very good 7X6 bull he killed in late November, 1984, with Orofino outfitter Ken Smith in Idaho's vast Selway Wilderness.

gration routes are. Some won't tell, however, so your next bet is to talk to Forest Service or Bureau of Land Management personnel who are familiar with the land administered by their agencies. Game wardens and biologists are also good sources of information.

During the late season, bulls lose their orneriness and get along nicely with one another. This is a departure from their early-fall behavior, when they dash around fighting for cows.

Because of their affability during this period, you might be rewarded with a herd of dandy bulls within shooting range. Your biggest chore is to figure which bull is largest and knock him down with a well-placed bullet. I've seen herds of two dozen bulls on the migration trail, any of which I'd have been proud to own.

To be successful during late season, you don't need to position yourself precisely next to the exact trail the elk use when they're traveling to winter range. In fact, most late-season hunting is a matter of tracking elk in snow. Except for the very late hunts I've already mentioned, most seasons will be over before the serious migration begins.

In most cases, when snow starts falling heavily, you should pursue elk as you would mule deer. The object is to spot animals as they're feeding, or to read sign in the snow, and proceed from there.

In Colorado, for example, two elk hunts are offered annually. An early season begins in mid-October, and a late season starts in early November. Hunters can choose only one season, and many gamble on good snow conditions for the late hunt. In much prime Colorado elk country, animals live in elevations from 9,000 to 10,000 feet or higher during the summer and fall. Heavy snows will get them moving down to elevations of 7,000 to 8,000 feet or lower, making them much more accessible to hunters. You don't need to know migration routes to score. If you can use binoculars and you aren't afraid to walk and look for tracks, your chances of tying a tag on an elk are just as good as anyone's.

These five lovely bulls are on winter range. After the rut they forget their differences and commonly band together in bull herds throughout late fall and winter.

During November, it's likely that you'll run across tracks made by large herds of elk. Although elk are always gregarious, they are more so in the late fall and winter when they gather in large groups to travel together. Tracking a herd of elk and sneaking within shooting range unseen is never easy, but it can be done, provided conditions are right. If the wind is wrong, the snow is noisy to walk on, or you have thick undergrowth to work through, your chances of getting close to a herd are slim to none.

Spotting a feeding herd of elk early in the morning and making a stalk is a good way to ensure success. Sometimes, however, cover is so sparse that it's tough to approach within shooting range. If that's the case, look over the country carefully and try to think like an elk. Since they'll probably spend the day bedded in timber, look for a logical bedding spot. Sneak over to the timber and position yourself where

Jack Atcheson took this excellent bull on winter range after snows drove the elk out of the high country.

you can see the feeding elk. If the strategy works, the elk will slowly move in your direction, and you can drop the animal of your choice. If the strategy fails and the elk go somewhere else to bed, you have two choices: You can either stalk them in their beds, or leave them alone for the day and ambush them late in the afternoon. If they aren't disturbed, they'll probably come back to feed in about the same spot. Get to your ambush spot early in the afternoon and be absolutely sure the wind is in your favor.

Don't overlook open, windswept ridges and slopes for elk. Animals often lay in the open if snow is deep in the general area around them. There's another way to find elk—listen for them. A big herd of elk is noisy. Cows and calves bark, squeal, and make noises that sound like mewing kittens. Bulls often bugle, even though they aren't supposed to during this period. On a calm day, you can hear an elk herd more than a mile away.

Don Laubach of Gardiner, Montana, stalks a bedded bull. This is not a trick photo. The bull was legal game and in a legal hunting unit. A hunter with a special late-season permit could have taken him.

To take advantage of this behavior, listen for elk when they're most active—in early morning and late afternoon. They'll be silent during the day when they're bedded. If you hear them, chances are good that they'll be in the open feeding. Glass for them from a high vantage point but be aware that they'll be difficult to locate. They're often not where you think they are, and sounds echoing and bouncing through the mountains can fool you.

Since snow and cold go hand in hand with late-season hunting, there's an inherent danger during this time of year. You might get caught in the middle of a horrid blizzard. Even a sturdy four-wheel-drive vehicle won't get you out of the boonies if a good ol' Rocky Mountain storm settles in. If it does you'll have to rely on a quick thaw, a snowplow, or good luck to get back to the blacktop.

It's a good idea to listen constantly for weather reports. If a severe storm warning with travel advisories is announced, get your camp out of the backcountry and set up close to an all-weather highway. There are plenty of places to hunt late-season elk near major highways.

Late-season elk hunting doesn't offer the romance of the early hunt, when bugling bulls tear around recklessly in search of cows. But remember, those same big bulls must evict their lofty lairs when deep snows pile up in the high country. If you play your cards right, one of those bulls might be yours.

CHAPTER 6

Is There a Perfect Elk Rifle?

Ken Smith peered over a knoll and spotted a herd of elk resting in a patch of alders. He eased his rifle to his shoulder, centered a bull in the scope, and squeezed the trigger. The bull shuddered at the report and crashed to the ground. Smith walked over and tagged a fine elk.

Smith is an outfitter from Orofino, Idaho. He's hunted elk all his life and has killed plenty of bulls. His choice of firearms is a .243, which surprises many elk hunters, yet Smith is unwavering in his respect for the .243.

"I know its limitations," he says. "I shoot only when I have the opportunity to place my bullet exactly where I want it. The .243 is deadly, but there's no room for error."

Bill Myers, an outfitter from Bozeman, Montana, sat in a clump of brush and blew into his bugle call. A bull responded and circled Myers carefully, trying to catch the hunter's scent. Myers spotted the bull in the trees, rested his .270 on a branch, and drilled the elk through both lungs. The .270 performed beautifully, and Myers recommends it highly for elk.

"The .270 has excellent ballistics and energy," Myers says. "It does the job for me in elk country, and that's all I ask. As in every other caliber, bullet placement is the most important factor, and the .270 is perfect medicine for any elk as long as the animal is hit right."

Billy Stockton, an outfitter from Wise River, Montana, shoots a .444 Marlin. He hunts thick timber almost exclusively and calls the .444 his "brush" gun.

"I hunt in close," Stockton says. "Most of my shots are under 100 yards, and the Marlin is just right. I haven't lost an elk yet, because I know where the gun shoots and I can hit what I want to. But I have a pretty strong opinion about

Billy Stockton, a veteran outfitter born and raised in big bull elk country along Montana's Big Hole River, uses a .444 Marlin Carbine for elk.

elk guns. It really doesn't matter what you shoot, as long as you can shoot it."

Smith, Myers, and Stockton share the same opinion, as do most hunters. An elk must be hit in a vital area, regardless of the caliber or bullet.

Ron Dube, an outfitter from Buffalo, Wyoming, feels the 7mm Mag is the answer to elk hunting. He uses it in Wyoming's high country where long shots are common, and likes the 7mm's flat-shooting capabilities.

"The 7mm Mag packs plenty of wallop," Dube says, "and that's an important aspect in elk hunting. A gun must have plenty of foot-pounds of energy to hurt an elk at long yardages."

Jack Atcheson of Butte, Montana, has seen 300 elk hit with bullets from all sorts of firearms. He is a strong proponent of heavyweight calibers and prefers the .338 for elk.

"I've seen too many elk wounded and unrecovered because hunters used firearms too light for the job," Atcheson said. "I believe in using a gun that delivers plenty of energy. The .338 is perfect, and I wouldn't use anything else."

Bruce Scott, an outfitter from Florence, Montana, doesn't believe in fooling with lightweight calibers either. He shoots a .45/70 with loads equivalent to a .458.

"When I hit an elk with a bullet, I want him down right now," Scott says. "I don't want him running off into some godforsaken canyon to die. It's tough enough to pack out an elk. There's no sense making it tougher. The .458 puts an elk to the ground as quick as anything. To me, that's important. And if I don't hit the elk quite right, the sheer destructive power of the big bullet will kill him quicker than a lightweight projectile."

Before debating the merits of elk rifles, we need to take a look at the elk.

The species is big, one of the biggest hooved animals in North America. A mature bull will weigh close to half a ton, and everything else about him is big as well. His bones are thick and heavy, his hide is tough, and he has a remarkable

Elk live in heavy timber, such as this bull, A gun must not only be up to the task of downing a big animal, but the hunter must be able to shoot it accurately as well.

tenacity. His stamina is incredible. That's a good reason for your rifle to be adequate for elk. It must be able to get the job done under all the circumstances you're likely to be confronted with in elk woods.

A bull elk's tenacity can be illustrated by an experience I had a few years ago. I was bugling into a draw from a clump of trees when a five-point bull dashed into the opening, obviously looking for a fight. I hit him through the lungs with a 180-grain Remington Core-Lokt, but the bull didn't know it. He raked a tree with his antlers, bugled, and I slipped another bullet into his vitals. That one took him down instantly. The first bullet was fatal, and the bull had only seconds to live, but his muscular frame and strength seemed to defy most anything.

A hunting buddy had an experience that also illustrates a bull's ability to take punishment. My friend was hunting

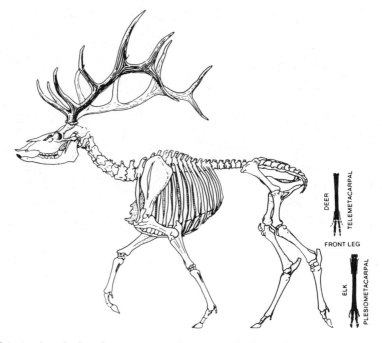

This is the skeletal structure of a prime bull elk. Note the position of the ribs and shoulder bone. This will give you an idea where to place your bullet, and the massive shoulder seems to suggest that you use a firearm up to the task of getting a projectile into a vital (illustration by A. B. Bubenik; courtesy of the Wildlife Management Institute).

in thick cover when he spotted a bull slowly walking in lodgepole pines about 100 yards away. The bull stopped and offered a clear chest shot through an opening in the trees. My pal sent a .308 bullet into the elk's left lung, but the bull stood still at the hit. Another shot hit the bull, but it remained rooted to the spot. After the third shot, the bull walked off, and 20 yards later it slumped to the ground. All three shots hit the lung area. A baseball could have covered the holes.

If we could always take our time and put a bullet into

an elk's vitals, then practically any high-powered rifle that delivers adequate foot-pounds of energy will be sufficient. But that's seldom the case these days. Elk are wilder than ever before, and your only glimpse might be a flash of tan fur in the timber. A spooked elk running in the trees is a tough target for any rifleman, no matter how good he is.

For that reason, a bullet needs to have plenty of energy to put the animal down if a perfect shot isn't made. And perfect shots will largely be the result of a lot of luck when you're trying to find an elk's vitals and everything is working against you.

An elk has a heavy shoulder bone, and I submit that this bone is the nemesis of all elk hunters. It will deflect bullets with insufficient energy, and is a superb protector of the vital area. I've seen a number of elk escape hunters after taking a hit in the shoulder, and I'm convinced that a firearm with more energy would have made a big difference. In most cases, .243's, 6mm's, and other lightweight rifles were used in those situations.

This is not to say that those calibers will not kill an elk. As I already indicated, several skilled outfitters respect the lightweight calibers, and they are convinced that their guns are up to the task.

A good way to start a spirited debate with your hunting buddies is to brag about the capabilities of your rifle and suggest that it's the finest instrument ever made for killing elk. Your companions will no doubt take serious exception to your foolish statement, and proceed to debate you on the subject. When the dust settles, no one will have convinced

A Remington 700. One of the most popular elk rifles on the market these days.

anyone else that any one rifle is indeed perfect. It's human nature to defend something that has performed for us in the past. As with anything else, we form allegiances toward products that get the job done.

My personal preference for elk is the .30/06, and only because I've used one for years. Yet, I've had experiences that suggest it might not be quite up to the task.

Jim Zumbo with a bull he took with ever-present Bertha, a pre-64 .30/06 Winchester Model 70 Featherwight. The author has taken more than 15 bulls with this rifle.

Several years ago, I had stalked close to a big seven-point bull on the Vermejo Park in New Mexico. I had been hunting for several days and passed up more than a dozen good elk in hopes of seeing a trophy-class animal. The bull I stalked was plenty good, bigger than anything I figured I'd see.

I waited more than 10 minutes before taking a shot because a small branch was directly in my line of fire. I didn't dare move for fear of spooking the bull, so I had to wait for him to take a step forward. He finally moved to where I had a clear shot, and my bullet took him squarely in the chest. The bull ran about 10 yards and stopped in the open. I shot again, and this time saw a small crimson spot where his lungs were. The elk looked directly at me after the shot, never showing signs of being hit. The third shot knocked him down, and I learned after looking him over that all three bullets had penetrated both lungs. I was using 165-grain Noslers in my Winchester Model 70 Featherweight .30/06. That rifle is my favorite; I use it for elk and deer without exception.

Technically, the elk was dead on his feet at the first shot, but I subscribe to the old addage that no elk is in the bag unless it's down on the ground. I might allow a fatally hit deer to falter and then drop, but an elk is too unpredictable.

The following year I hit a five-point bull twice in the chest while hunting in Colorado. After the second shot, he walked 10 yards and collapsed. Both bullets took him in the lungs.

A year later I was hunting with Bruce Scott in Idaho. Bruce called up a big six-point bull with a bugle call, and I hit him in the lungs at the first shot. The bull staggered, ran forward several yards, and stood still. I maneuvered myself around until I could get another clear shot in the timber, and drilled him again. The bull lurched forward, still on his feet. After several shots, all in the chest area, the bull finally toppled over.

A few months afterward, I hit a five-point bull in the lungs during a late hunt in Montana. He ran 200 yards before he died.

These incidents seem to suggest that the .30/06 is a marginal elk rifle. That's possible, but I think it's an adequate caliber, and it gets my vote as being the best. That's a biased opinion, of course, but the rifle gets the job done. While it's true that many elk don't drop to their feet at the first shot, I've never lost one. The deep penetration by the 165-grain Nosler partition bullets insures that the projectile won't prematurely explode when striking a heavy bone or rib.

I won't go so far as to say that the .30/06 is the answer as far as elk rifles go, however. It's fine for me because it works and I'm confident with it. The rifle is an old friend. I know every scratch and nick, and if I miss or shoot poorly it's always my fault.

I think that's the most important aspect of measuring a firearm's capabilities. If it delivers enough energy and is reasonably flat-shooting, a rifle should be up to the task of performing well for you in the elk woods. If you're comfortable with the gun and shoot it accurately, stay with it. Don't be swayed by stories that suggest that only heavy magnums should be used on elk, unless you can shoot those heavy magnums. Excessive recoil can be your worst enemy. If you're afraid of the firearm, you won't shoot well with it, no matter how powerful it is. Better to use something you can handle without fear.

I'm sure that many of the elk I've tagged would have gone down at the first shot if I'd been using a big magnum. My .30/06 has claimed 15 elk, and none escaped after being hit initially. That's what counts, though some elk had to be followed and located after they ran off and died after being hit. You could use bowhunting as a comparision. Once a lethal shot is made, some tracking will no doubt be required.

If you want the quarry down quickly, however, you'll need at least a 7mm Mag, and preferably a .300 Mag or .338

Mag. Of course, any caliber will tip an elk over instantly if the animal is hit in the right spot. A .22 bullet will kill a bull if the projectile smacks it between the eyes and penetrates the skull into the brain. Choice of firearms is up to you. And even then an elk might not cooperate.

Another important consideration is long-range capability. Though you might be hunting heavy timber with close shots expected, there's always the chance that you'll see a bull across a draw or in an opening that's a good distance away. Remember that light calibers quickly lose energy beyond 300 yards. They might be flat-shooting and superb for antelope or deer, but by the time they hit big elk at long yardages, they won't have enough punch to hurt the animals. It's fine to debate muzzle velocity and muzzle energy, but that's not pertinent to hunting. Foot-pounds are the all-important factor, and they must be sufficient out there where the elk is standing or running, not at the muzzle or in between. I'd be wary of any firearm that doesn't deliver at least 1800 foot-pounds at the point of impact.

More and more hunters seem to lean toward bigger bores for elk these days. If any one caliber is showing up more than others, it's the 7mm Mag. Some hunters feel it's the very minimum caliber to use. Let's take a look at the ballistics of the 7mm Mag.

The popular 150-grain pointed bullet shows a velocity of 2568 feet per second and an energy of 2196 foot-pounds at

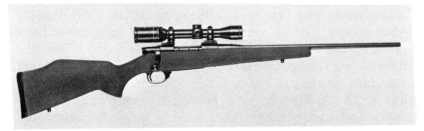

A Weatherby Fiberguard Rifle. A nice choice for the elk hunter. It's light, has a short barrel, and is available in several excellent calibers.

200 yards. The 175-grain boattail zings out at 2580 fps with a hard-hitting energy factor of 2586 foot-pounds at 200 yards. That's plenty of promise and power. When compared to my .30/06, only a .30/06 200-grain boattail bullet has energy to exceed the 150-grain 7mm Mag at 200 yards, and nothing in the .30/06 bullet line can touch the energy of the 175-grain boattail in 7mm Mag.

Besides energy and trajectory, an elk hunter needs to consider the ability of a bullet to penetrate the thick hide and muscles to get the job done. This means a bullet of sufficient jacket thickness to hold together long enough to get deep into vital areas. It must not explode upon contact with the hide or the first bone it strikes, a common problem with lightweight, thin-skinned bullets.

Aside from the rifle's capability of killing an elk, you should pay attention to its weight. In typical elk country you'll be doing a great deal of walking, unless you can ride a horse. Even so, the horse will get you into places where elk live, but you'll likely spend a lot of time afoot. Every extra pound on your rifle will make the hunt a bigger ordeal.

My Featherweight weighs exactly 8½ pounds, including sling, scope, and a full magazine. Every now and then I've hefted 9½- and 10-pound firearms for comparison, and was amazed at the difference. You shouldn't have any problem selecting a lightweight rifle these days. Most major manufacturers are introducing light firearms.

Optics are also an important part of an elk rifle. Though many westerners still use open sights, most hunters prefer a scope. I like a four-power scope and have never been enamored by the variable models. The variable offers the option of high magnification for seeing detail, but I use my binoculars for that purpose. If I had to choose a variable, I'd want a 3X-9X Model. As a rule, I'd shoot using the low powers since high magnification only increases unwanted rifle movement because it makes it seem more unsteady.

A good waterproof scope is important, since wet weather is always likely in the West, even though most moisture is in the form of snow. If you're hunting Roosevelt's elk along the West Coast, however, rainy weather is normal. Scope caps are a good idea to keep the lens free of moisture.

Whatever kind of gun you use for elk hunting, keep in mind the all-important aspect of becoming familiar with your rifle. You can own the finest machine ever made for killing elk, but if you can't shoot it, it's worthless.

If you're in doubt about the caliber and aren't concerned about recoil and noise, I'd lean to the heavy side. Remember that the quarry is big and tough. Those extra foot-pounds might spell the difference between success and failure when everything is working against you. And when you're elk hunting, you can count on most everything to go wrong. Those so-called perfect shots at a motionless elk standing in the open are few and far between. Be prepared for any eventuality, and use a gun that will do the job. You owe it to the elk.

CHAPTER 7

Optics for Elk

A friend once made an interesting statement. "Elk are so big," he said, "they must look like horses in the forest. Why are they so tough to hunt?"

My pal was from the east and had never hunted the West. "Just wait, good buddy," I responded, "you'll see why they're so tough to hunt when you try it."

And he did. And now he knows. His opinion of elk changed remarkably during our 10-day hunt.

The fact that elk are big doesn't mean that they're easily visible. To hunt successfully, we need an assist from optical equipment. A hunter who pursues elk without optics is asking for trouble. I can think of only one exception, and that's when a hunter has an either-sex tag and is pussyfooting around in dense timber such as in West Coast forests inhabited by Roosevelt's elk or even heavily timbered places where Rocky Mountain elk live. In those cases, elk are often spotted up close, and the either-sex tag doesn't require identification of sex. Anything wearing elk fur is legal quarry.

But even in those situations, optics are an important asset. More than once I've seen a patch of elk, wondering if I

These hunters take time to glass for elk in Utah high country. A big part of elk hunting is glassing in the early morning and late afternoon hours when elk are feeding.

was looking at the chest, paunch, or hindquarter. Optics will help you fit those jigsaw pieces together and identify what you're looking at.

Elk that aren't in heavy timber are not easy to spot, either. Their brown and yellow bodies blend in well with natural surroundings. You can usually figure on elk being out of sight about 95 percent of the time anyway. Most of their feeding in the open occurs at night or around the edges of darkness. That's when optics are most valuable. Poor light is the period of high elk activity. Anything that can help you see animals during that time will give you a great advantage.

I'm never without a set of binoculars around my neck, and a spotting scope is always close by. My rifle wears a scope as well.

Binoculars come in a wide variety of sizes, models, and

This bull is almost hidden in vegetation. A riflescope will help pinpoint the shot, and binoculars would help see him.

capabilities. It's difficult to choose from the large assortment available. Don't let low prices affect your decision when perusing binoculars. Buy the best glasses you can afford, and only from reputable firms. You might never forgive yourself if you buy a cheap pair and have them fail you during the moment of truth in the elk woods.

If you're looking at questionable binoculars, never buy them from a discount mail-order house. Make your decision only after you've looked through them. That means you'll likely purchase them at a sporting goods store. Ask the clerk if you can test them outside the store, preferably when the light is poor.

The basic binocular has two prismatic-erecting telescopes that appear as one when placed to the eyes. Prisms are used to place the image into normal viewing position.

Porro prisms are most common in binoculars and account for the offset profile of many binocular systems. The roof prism is being used rather than the porro in new models to eliminate the offset housing, which decreases bulk and weight in the binocular and also creates a new design.

The twin binocular tubes are connected by a hinge so they can be adjusted to fit different eyes. Some binoculars are focused by turning the eyepieces on each cylinder separately, and fortunately they've gone the way of the Edsel. Most glasses have a single wheel between the two barrels, or a flat lever that is pressed down to make focal adjustments.

Most binoculars have some sort of eyepiece device to allow eyeglass wearers to look squarely into the tubes. The standard design is a simple rubber ring that can be rolled in or out, depending on the need.

Binoculars are classified by two sets of figures, as in 7X35, 6X30, etc. The first figure is the magnifying power;

Cut-away view shows Bausch & Lomb's porro prism binocular.

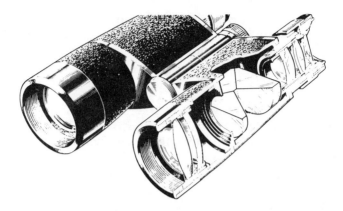

Cuy-away view illustrates Bushnell's roof prism binocular.

the second refers to the diameter of the objective lens in millimeters. The objective lens is the one farthest from the eye, in front of the barrel. The rear lens closest to the eye is the ocular lens.

"Relative brightness," which is vital to the hunter, is the relationship of power to the diameter of the objective lens, and is figured thusly: Divide the diameter of the objective lens by the power, square the result, and you have relative brightness. For example, a 7X35 would have a relative brightness of 25. This is obtained by dividing 7 into 35, which equals 5, and 5 squared is 25. You have the same relative brightness with 6X30's and 8X40's, since all come to 5 when divided, with a result of 25 when squared. A 7X50, however, would divide out to 7.1 and have a relative brightness of 50.4. Obviously, this binocular has superior light-gathering power in poor light.

When using the binoculars, you'll notice that the higher the magnification, the more the view wavers. The binoculars aren't causing the waver, it just details the object more clearly and you see movement better.

The best binoculars for elk country should offer a crisp focus, have good relative brightness, and be lightweight. The last element is important. Elk hunting is different than most other forms of hunting because you won't be hunting much from a vehicle. There are exceptions, but by and large you'll be walking, climbing, squeezing through timber, or riding a horse. You'll want lightweight binoculars that will be almost unnoticeable when you're wearing them.

Some hunters figure a riflescope will double as a set of binoculars. Not only is that bad logic, it's dangerous. Safety rules absolutely demand that you not aim a rifle at something you can't identify, and that's what you'll be doing if you see movement or a suspicious object and try to view it through a scope. It could very well be another hunter.

From a practical standpoint, a scope allows you to scan with only one eye instead of two as you'd be doing with binoculars. Additionally, you need to go through the motions of finding a good rest for your rifle to steady the scope, and that's not always possible when the situation warrants it.

William H. Nesbitt, left, Administrative Director of the Boone and Crockett Club, and two other hunters glass the Colorado countryside early in the morning.

In my way of thinking, riflescopes are a mandatory part of every serious elk hunter's equipment list. There are some notable exceptions, however, and those involve close-in situations in which the range is short. Billy Stockton, my good outfitter buddy from Wise River, Montana, has killed more big bulls with an open-sighted .444 Marlin carbine than many hunters will see in a lifetime. Billy gets away with it because he was raised in elk country and is savvy to the ways of bulls. Most of us need the advantage of a scope.

Elsewhere in this book, I've said that elk are timber-oriented animals. They spend most of the daylight hours nestled in a dense stand of trees or brush and come out into the open when light starts to fade in the afternoon, and when night starts to fade in the morning. Nonetheless, don't figure on most of your opportunities being in the timber. Most of the shots I've made at elk were in the 150- to 200-yard range, and one of the biggest bulls I ever took required a 400-plus-yard shot. I would have been in big trouble with plenty of elk if I had had open sights.

Scopes are classified by power, which usually ranges from 2X up to 20X or higher. I use a 4X for all my big game hunting and only for nostalgic reasons. When I graduated from college, my father-in-law bought me a Model 70 Winchester .30/06 topped with a Weaver 4X scope as a gift. I've used that rifle for 22 years for most of my big game hunting, including elk, and haven't been unhappy.

Variable models are common these days and are fine in the elk woods. The most popular types are the 3X-9X models, and Simmons Optics has come out with an interesting 4X-1OX.

Other reputable models include the Bushnell Scopechief 3X-9X IV and the Leupold Vari-X 3X-9X. Redfield's Wide-field model gives an extra-wide field of view.

When using variable scopes, most hunters prefer to shoot at low power and use the high power for greater magnification when looking over an animal's antlers, etc.

Author uses lightweight binoculars, They're easy to carry and optics are adequate for all elk hunting situations.

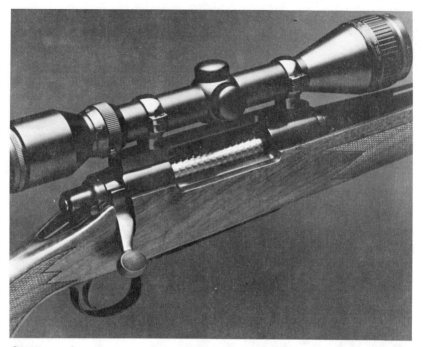

Simmons has just put this 4X10 scope and the market and it has all the makings of a superb glass for elk.

Scopes are often coated to reduce sun glare, and some have special light-gathering qualities. The latter factor is important when trying to make a shot in low-light conditions. I'd strongly advise using a scope that has superior light-gathering capabilities. It can spell the difference between going home with an unused tag or a quarter-ton of elk meat.

The reticle is the visible system within the scope that allows you to pinpoint the target. Plain crosshairs have been the most popular, and others include the post, dot, and various combinations. Some scopes have range finders built within that allow you to estimate range, and some compensate for bullet drop. If you purchase a scope with these fea tures, be sure you are intimately familiar with it at all ranges. Don't draw the bead on an elk and wonder where to

This 3X9 scope by Burris is a fine choice for a varipowered scope and is a quality brand as well.

hold. To do so might result in a missed animal, or worse, a wounded one.

Waterproof and fogproof scopes are a must in elk country. Moisture is always a possibility, especially snow. In the coastal forests, rain is a fact of life.

Your scope will probably take a beating as you climb and hike, and you'll be shoving and pulling it in and out of scabbards. Make sure it is durable and can be battered without affecting its accuracy.

You'll likely drive or fly a good distance to your elk hunt. There's always a chance that the vibration from an airplane or vehicle will alter your scope's adjustment. If possible, fire the rifle and test it before heading into camp. In the event that you're in game country and don't want to fire a shot, but you think your scope might have been knocked out of adjustment, you can quickly bore-sight it to see if it's basically on target.

To do this, remove the bolt so you can look down the bore, and set a target at the distance at which you've sighted-in the rifle. Carefully rest the rifle on a solid surface that will couch it comfortably but firmly, aim the bore at the target by looking through it, and very carefully raise your eye to the scope to see if the scope is pointed at the target. If

A spotting scope has practical usage in western hunting, despite its bulk and weight. Many elk hunters use them to glass long ranges or to inspect distant antlers for trophy quality.

it is, the scope alignment is probably acceptable, although this test isn't as accurate as you'd like it to be. If the bore and scope don't match, you've got big troubles. Resight the rifle, even if you have to go some distance to do it.

Spotting scopes are basically telescopes used for hunting. Because they take a beating, spotting scopes are usually constructed so they can be handled roughly.

The weight and bulk of a spotting scope precludes carrying them long distances, but serious trophy hunters use them extensively. They're handy for sizing up the antlers of a distant elk, and they're also handy for spotting elk in the first place.

Several years ago, I was hunting with a pal who had a tag for a quality elk unit in Utah. I didn't have a tag, so I sat under a shady tree eating a sandwich while my friend glassed a patch of junipers with a spotting scope. We had seen some elk run into the general area several hours earlier, but the sun had risen high in the sky and we knew they'd be bedded in the trees somewhere. I was about to tell my buddy to quit straining his eyes when he motioned me to come over. Remarkably, he had located a cow elk standing in a tiny opening. He made a superb stalk and killed a six-point bull in its bed.

Because of their high magnification, spotting scopes must be used on either a tripod or a mount that clamps to a vehicle window. Tripods are compact and fold into a small size.

The magnification of spotting scopes ranges from 15X to 65X, with 20X being one of the most popular. Several models are rubber coated for durability, and I recommend them highly for an elk hunt. Simmons Optics has an innovative scope that has a small 2X lens mounted on the barrel to help find the target quickly. Once the quarry is located in the small lens, you simply move your eye to the main lens.

Optics are exceedingly important on your elk hunt. Pay attention to them, and use them properly. They can make or break your hunt.

CHAPTER 8

Hunting Elk with a Bow

Hunting with a bow and arrow is the supreme challenge when it comes to pursuing elk. Nothing else compares with it. The quarry is big and tough, and it lives in a vast landscape that is as rugged as any in North America.

If there's a saving grace, it's the biological fact that elk are in the rut when most bow seasons occur. That means you can call elk in with a bugle (if you're good enough, and in the right place at the right time, and if the elk cooperate).

Another chapter details bugling techniques, so I won't go into them again. But there's a vast difference between shooting an elk with a bow and with a rifle, no matter how close and worked up he is.

One of the biggest headaches for the bowhunter is the amount of wood and foliage between the arrow and the elk. Whereas a rifleman can thread the needle, so to speak, and slip a bullet through a myriad of twigs, branches, and tree trunks, the archer must have more air to work with.

An arrow in flight, whether it be wood, glass, or aluminum, has as much ability to punch through obstacles as I have of licking a mad grizzly with my bare hands. The

Jim Teeny, a well-known west coast fly fisherman, poses proudly with a fine Oregon bull. Teeny has bow-killed 9 elk in 9 years.

Jim Teeny packs his bull's head out of the Oregon forest.

slightest solid objects, be they leaves or twigs, will destroy an arrow's ballistics and cause it to deflect.

Now then, I'm not going to pretend I'm a skilled bowhunter and write this chapter as an expert. The truth is, I've killed one bull elk with a bow in my life, exactly two months prior to writing this book. I killed a mule deer 20 years ago with an arrow, and I'm not qualified to inform and entertain you with all sorts of interesting personal anecdotes. But I'll do my best to pass on what I've learned as well as tips from friends who are indeed experts.

Keep in mind another important fact. You can be a tournament champion archer, but that doesn't mean you'll kill an elk. You've got to understand elk behavior and know how to hunt the big animals. I know several highly skilled archers who have yet to kill their first elk because they don't have woods savvy.

As any experienced bowhunter will tell you, practice is of utmost importance. You must become intimately familiar with your equipment, and you must learn how to shoot accurately. But there's another must, and one that many hunters ignore: learn how to quickly estimate distances.

The flight trajectory of an arrow is horrible. The shaft is quickly obedient to the laws of gravity and allows little margin of error. A misjudgment of just five yards or less may result in a clean miss, even an easy shot that you would have made had you calculated the distance correctly.

When hunting elk, you won't have much time to determine yardage. An animal may give you just a quick shot as it steps between two trees or a small opening. Your shot will probably be close in—30 yards or less—but you should be prepared for longer shots. I've imposed a 50-yard limit on myself, and won't shoot at anything beyond that.

If you're hunting during the bugle period and will call elk, make some preparations before you call. Larry D. Jones, who manufactures one of the finest assortments of elk bugle calls in the country and is an expert bowhunter, always clears several shooting lanes in an area before calling. He allows for wind direction and tries to figure which way the bull will come in. When satisfied with three or four lanes, he makes his call.

Larry doesn't take his stand behind a deadfall, blowdown, bush, or other type of natural screen. He stands in front of it and uses plenty of camo to allow himself to blend in well. He stands in front of vegetation so that he has more room to maneuver his bow and shoot through trees.

It's important to be able to draw your bow unhindered by surrounding branches and foliage. If you have to shoot from a contorted position, chances are that you won't anchor the arrow correctly and will miss the target. Before you call, draw the bowstring back to full draw from several positions to make sure you have enough freedom of movement. If you don't, clear away the offending branch or move to a different calling position.

When you practice before the hunt, try shooting from different angles. Many field ranges are set up so you have to shoot uphill, downhill, between trees, through branches, and from various stances. If no such range is available, take your bow to the woods and practice shooting at different objects. Be sure your practice arrows weigh the same as your hunting broadheads, because any variation can cause you to shoot differently.

While actually hunting, you should shoot at various objects during lulls in the day. Keep a practice arrow in your quiver, and constantly try to hit targets at various yardages. An anthill, sandy bank, or a stick in a meadow make good targets. Don't shoot at stumps or trees, or you'll end up burying your arrow in wood.

Your choice of bows is entirely up to you. If you're typical, you'll choose one of the new compounds and use aluminum arrows. I shoot a Golden Eagle bow and find it well suited to my needs.

Compound bows have just about taken over the bowhunting market, though some hunters use recurves and even longbows. My good friend, Max Stewart of Vernal,

Clare Conley, Editor of OUTDOOR LIFE magazine, takes practice shots outside camp during a break in the hunting.

Although most bowhunters use compound bows, a growing number are going back to more primitive equipment as this hunter who uses a longbow.

Utah, shoots a longbow and amazes friends with his accuracy. He calls it his "black-powder bow" and easily competes with archers who use compounds equipped with bowsights.

If you buy a compound bow, have it adjusted to a comfortable draw weight, and increase the weight as desired when you can handle it. Be sure to purchase arrows correctly sized to your draw. Many sporting goods dealers will assist you in determining your draw length. I use the same arrows for practice and hunting, and simply exchange heads as required.

There are many different types of broadheads on the market. You'll find staunch support among experienced bowhunters for just about every style. Be sure your arrows are razor sharp.

As I've said elsewhere in this book, elk have big bones and tough hides. If you don't get your arrow into a vital area and cause damage, you won't fill your tag. An elk is big enough that you might lose sight of the need to place your arrow into his chest. Believe me, there's plenty of room to miss on an elk. A poor shot may result in a wounded animal that might not be recovered. Never release an arrow unless you're positive you can hit the elk in the critical vital spot. You might be tempted to try a marginal shot because of the intervening vegetation, but don't do it.

As with all big game animals, any movement on your part may betray your presence and alert an elk. If you're calling, keep an arrow nocked and position your bow so you can ease it up. When an elk is coming in to a bugle call, he's often so worked up that he'll stop and demolish a small tree or bush with his antlers. This is the time to bring up your bow and get ready for the shot. If you're using a compound and a shot is imminent, you can come to full draw and hold the arrow for several seconds until the elk is where you want him. You'll find this tough to do with a conventional recurve, which is a chief reason for the compound's popularity.

I killed my elk in Montana with Billy Stockton, a long-

Jim Zumbo with his first bow-killed elk, taken in Montana in 1984.

time friend. Billy called the elk in from a long distance, and I was positioned behind a log at the edge of a meadow. As the elk approached, I crouched low and watched the antlers of the five-point bull as it slowly walked along below me. He was headed straight to Billy, completely unaware of my presence.

I drew the arrow back to full draw when the elk's head was below the curve of the slope, and then I slowly raised up. He never saw me as I sent the arrow deep into his chest. We found him dead 60 yards away, and learned that the arrow penetrated both lungs and the top of his heart.

I learned a valuable lesson on that hunt. By teaming up with another person who is calling, you can ambush an elk much more easily. The bull is responding to the caller, and if the wind is right, has no idea that you're in the country. The caller actually becomes a decoy as well as an attractor.

Many hunters pursue elk solo and don't have the advantage of teaming up. In that case, it's smart to learn how to use the diaphragm call which fits inside your mouth. Your hands are free to wield the bow, and you won't have to make any unnecessary moves to blow the call or take it away from your mouth. Larry Jones, as well as other manufacturers, produces diaphragm calls. The best way to learn to use them is to buy one of Jones' instructional tapes, or tapes produced by other elk call companies.

If you aren't bowhunting during the bugle season, you'll have your work cut out for you. It's tough to get close to an elk, especially since they usually band together in herds and live in heavily timbered country that is generally noisy to move around in.

In Utah the elk bowhunt is held in August, long before the rut. Some hunters have scored by watching wallows from tree stands. Wallows are mudholes or springs that elk roll around in during late summer. You can usually tell if animals are using a wallow by noting the freshness of tracks in the mud. I've found that elk often visit wallows late in the afternoon, usually just before dark.

Craig Doherty with a tremendous bull taken in 1984. This bull
will be included in Montana's top 25 bow-killed elk.

If you're hunting in an arid area, watching a waterhole from a tree stand or ground blind might work, but be prepared to spend a long time there. Elk generally water just before shooting light is gone or during the night.

In the event that you spot elk feeding in a meadow, you might try setting up an ambush in the afternoon or the next morning. It's not a good idea to try a stalk, unless you're sure you can move in the timber and approach the edge of the trees without spooking the herd. If undisturbed, elk often return to the same feeding area day after day. By noting the route they take to and from their bedding spot in the timber, you might be able to locate their trail in the forest and set up on it early in the morning as they leave the meadow, or late in the afternoon as they leave bedding areas.

Stillhunting is a poor way to hunt elk with a bow if the landscape is thickly vegetated. You'll have a tough time finding animals, and when you do, you'll have a tougher time approaching within bow range. Trying a shot at a bedded elk is never a good idea, because too often the vital area is unexposed as the animal is lying down.

Of course, the bottom line in bowhunting is getting close to the quarry. Since most states offer bowhunts during the elk rut, you'll have a superb chance of drawing one in close. Sometimes *too* close. I know bowhunters who have had elk so close that they could have touched them with their bow.

You have an excellent opportunity of taking a record-class elk with a bow because of its vulnerability during the breeding season. In fact, hunting can be so outstanding that few states have firearm hunts during the rut. Those that have them do restrict gun hunting to wilderness or back-country areas.

Now that I've taken my first bull with a bow, which, incidentally, was the first year I ever tried it, you can be assured that I'll be trying it a whole lot more. It's a superb way to hunt and is elk hunting's toughest challenge.

CHAPTER 9

Muzzleloading for Elk

Elk hunting is always a challenge, regardless of the time of year you're pursuing elk or the circumstances of the hunt. The ultimate challenge is trying for them with a bow, but the odds are tipped toward the hunter a bit because most bowhunts are held during the bugle season and it's possible to call a bull in close. The muzzleloader hunter, to be sure, is also faced with a tough challenge, because he or she has but one shot, the animal must be close, and the accuracy of the gun cannot be compared with the high technology optics and rifles we use during regular firearms seasons.

Muzzleloaders are called primitive weapons by most observers because they're remnants of early America when pioneers settled the land and soldiers fought to win independence. Only one shot was offered to the shooter, and the ball had to be on the mark because a second chance was unlikely.

And so it is today, except that we aren't fighting the British or Indians or grizzly bears. A quick second shot doesn't mean life or death, but its absence means the first one has to be good. I don't know many elk that will let you fumble around with a gun for several seconds if you've taken a shot and missed.

Though the one-shot requirement is a challenge anticipated by many muzzleloader hunters, there are other reasons for participating in the sport.

One is the timing of the hunt. Some states offer special muzzleloader seasons or hunts that are far superior to general firearms seasons. Colorado, for example, holds its regular firearms seasons after the bugle period. Not so with the muzzleloader hunt. The season starts in September, smack in the middle of the rut.

Another attraction to the sport is the esthetic appeal. To many modern rifle hunters, a gun is a tool, an impersonal bit of metal, wood, and plastic that is taken out of the gun case a few times a year and used when required.

Not so with the majority of muzzleloader hunters. The piece is caressed, fondled, and treated with ever-loving care. In fact, many muzzleloader hunters buy kits and put their guns together part by part.

Besides the gun, other sundry items are required to participate in the sport. A possibles bag holds balls, powder, patches, percussion caps, and all sorts of goodies needed to fire the weapon. Besides the bag, which is usually carried on a strap over the shoulder, a number of objects dangle from other straps and laces as well. A short-start, ball and cap holders, and other accoutrements decorate the hunter. And if the gunbearer is hard-core, he or she will be wearing authentic buckskin clothing complete with authentic campfire odors, a coon, skunk, or coyote cap, mocassins, beard, beads, buffalo robe, and maybe an earring or two.

None of these folks look alike. Each has individual preferences, and their apparel is refreshingly original. And when there is a break in the hunting day or the campfire coals glow in the blackness, the conversation is generally directed toward mountain men, their guns, and their lifestyles.

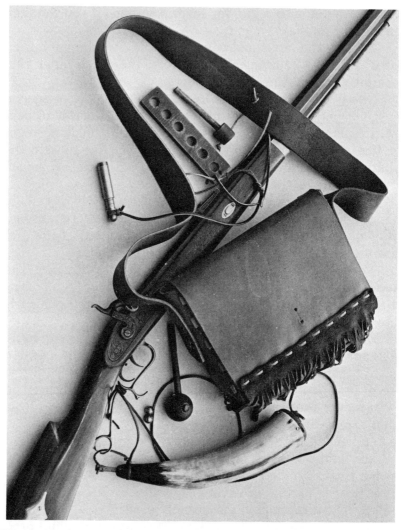

This is standard equipment for the muzzleloader. Much of this gear is homemade, which is typical of black-powder hunters. (Photo courtesy of Jerry Horgesheimer).

Whether you follow the traditions or simply enjoy shooting muzzleloaders for their own sake, elk are superb quarry. They live in the timber most of the day and are approachable within short range if you hunt correctly. Besides the disadvantage of having only one shot and the need to get close, you'll be using open sights as well.

I should mention that some muzzleloaders install scopes on their guns. I believe that defeats the purpose of the sport and, fortunately, only a few hunters do it.

Let's take a close look at the firearm. It gets its name because it's loaded from the muzzle rather than from the rear. The firearms are also described as black-powder rifles, front-loaders, and in the vernacular, smokepoles and front-stuffers.

Muzzleloaders are different from modern-day rifles because the shooter must put together various components to get a shot off. Whereas the contemporary rifleman slips a self-contained cartridge into a gun and shoots it, the muzzleloader hunter must insert powder, patch and ball, or greased bullet into the chamber, ram the projectile into place with a rod, and affix a percussion cap or add powder to a flintlock. Not surprisingly, this process is tended to with a great deal of imagination in some cases, with all kinds of helpful gadgets to help speed the process. And, of course, every hunter has his pet load, ball, or bullet, and the array of possibilities is endless.

Muzzleloaders became popular in the United States in the mid-1950's. At that time, Navy Arms Company and Centennial Arms Corporation entered the market, and were soon followed by other manufacturers, giving birth to a brand-new sport that spread like wildfire.

There are two basic muzzleloader styles: percussion or caplock guns, and flintlocks. The former is the most popular, because it's more reliable, easier to use, and is generally less expensive.

In the caplock models, a cap containing a fulminate of

mercury is placed on the nipple, and the cap ignites when struck by the hammer. The spark travels through a vent hole and ignites the powder charge behind the ball or bullet.

The flintlock requires a different system. Instead of using a cap, a small amount of fine powder is poured into the flash pan. A chunk of flint attached to the descending hammer strikes the steel or frizzen, and the ensuing spark ignites the powder in the flash pan. The spark travels through the touchhole and into the chamber where it ignites the powder charge behind the projectile.

It becomes readily apparent that any muzzleloader must be in perfect working condition to fire. A blocked vent, wet powder, malfunctioning cap or flint can stymie the shot. As a result, you might be looking at an elk across the sights and pull the trigger on a nonperforming gun. At that point you might as well throw rocks at the animal, scream invectives, or just sit down on a log and cry. Most elk will not allow you to figure out what's wrong with your dud gun.

How effective are black-powder guns on elk? If you can shoot well with a muzzleloader and can get within the range that you're comfortable with, you should be able to tip over any bull that walks.

Some people claim black-powder firearms are too inaccurate to use for big game hunting, and others say they're so accurate that it's unfair to use them during special seasons when elk hunting is at its best.

I think both opinions are exaggerated. A muzzleloader is effective, but it has limitations. There's plenty of room for error, but an experienced shooter should be able to hit the target with reasonable accuracy. I've seen some expert shooters work wonders with black-powder rifles, but they're the exception.

As in other forms of hunting, practice is the only answer to becoming a skilled shooter. No one should carry a muzzleloader unless he or she can consistently punch holes through a target at whatever maximum range the hunter has settled on. That might be 75, 100, 150 yards or even more.

Can a muzzleloading rifle kill a big bull like this that might weigh upwards of 800 pounds? You bet—black-powder firearms are lethal weapons as long as hunters use them within limits.

The most popular black-powder calibers are .36, .45, .50, .54, and .58. Elk hunters generally use .54's and .58's or higher. The .50 caliber is perhaps the most popular big game caliber, but I'd opt for something bigger for elk.

To the inexperienced hunter, black-powder firearms are

strange weapons. The belching cloud of smoke and flying sparks are foreign but necessary occurrences, and the various accessories as well as the nomenclature are unfamiliar and confusing.

I was half terrified the first time I fired a muzzleloader. I loaded my new flintlock with a minimum charge and politely let my pal shoot it first. When the smoke cleared and I realized my friend was still alive, I loaded the gun, half-closed my eyes, and squeezed the trigger. The resulting explosion within inches of my face unnerved me, and a quick inspection of my face revealed no blood or third-degree burns. The rest was easy. I fired the gun until I ran out of powder, and now I chuckle when I think about my early fears.

Once you learn the basics, you'll soon be wanting to know all you can about muzzleloaders. You'll no doubt buy or make a possibles bag and load it with equipment.

A big challenge will be to reload the second shot quickly. You'll get better and faster as you practice. In some cases, a second shot at an elk will present itself, and you'll want to be ready as soon as possible. Percussion cap holders allow you to quickly slip a cap on a nipple in one fluid motion, and you can use predetermined powder charges instead of taking time to measure and load. You can also use precut patches that don't have to be sliced off after the ball is seated, and you can ram pregreased bullets down the muzzle and not fool with patches and balls.

You might consider joining a black-powder group or befriend a muzzleloader enthusiast who might share tips and techniques. For detailed instructions on all phases of black-powder hunting, read one of the many excellent books on the subject.

Black powder itself is classed into four different ratings: Fg (largest), FFg, FFFg, and FFFFg (smallest). That's about it. Whereas the modern rifleman can choose from a large variety of powders and loads, and fusses over scales and precision equipment, the muzzleloader hunter worries only

Muzzleloading hunters acquire a unique camaraderie. Much time is spent discussing firearms, accessories, hunting traditions, and even clothing.

about one or two powders and simply shakes more or less into the muzzle of his gun as required. Besides black powder, a substance called Pyrodex is used by many hunters. It's safer to use than black powder, is just as effective, and is immune to red tape and regulations applied to black powder.

Although round balls are commonly used by many muzzleloader hunters, Maxi and Mini balls and bullets are popular as well. Your preference will depend on your growing familiarity with the gun. As you become more experienced, you'll select a projectile that works best for you.

Be aware that black powder is highly dangerous. You must follow safety precautions when using it.

Briefly, never smoke when handling it. A hot ash could

cause an explosion, and if the ash falls onto a loaded flash pan of a flintlock, the gun could fire.

Never pour powder from a flask or powderhorn directly into a hot barrel, because if there are any hot grains of powder in the gun it could ignite the fresh charge and turn your flask or horn into a bomb. Always pour powder from a measure.

If the gun misfires, wait several seconds before examining it. Otherwise a latent spark could trigger ignition when you don't expect it.

Never use any substance other than black powder or Pyrodex in your muzzleloader. Smokeless powder is made for modern cartridges, never for a muzzleloader.

When you hunt elk with a primitive gun, you'll have your work cut out for you unless you can hunt during the rut. If you can do so, learn how to bugle effectively. Chances are good you won't have much company from other hunters, which is a nice advantage of using muzzleloaders.

If you must hunt after the rut, use your stillhunting talents to get close to animals. Remember the limitations of your gun, and don't expect it to work wonders. You'll need to place the ball precisely, because you won't have the advantage of high energies and velocities of high-powered bullets.

Don't be surprised if the muzzleloader fever catches up with you and claims you as a member of the growing fraternity of black-powder hunters. The sport is intriguing; it won't take much to win you over if you love the challenge of the hunt.

CHAPTER 10

The Trophy Elk

A hunter once told me that there's no such thing as a nontrophy bull elk. Every one is a trophy, he said, regardless of the dimensions of its antlers.

I have no quarrel with that attitude. I've yet to lament *any* elk I've shot, whether it was a mediocre four-point or a spike bull. But for the purposes of this chapter, let's discuss monster bulls—the kind that give you the shakes and cause your heart to pound.

Actually, any elk with antlers will cause those aforementioned conditions. A monster to one person might be just so-so to another. I remember a hunt in Wyoming that illustrates this phenomenon.

Several hunters were positioned around a thick stand of spruces, waiting for elk to burst out of the trees. A half-dozen guides were walking about in the timber, trying to rout elk out to the standers. I was one of the standers, and though I don't put much faith in elk drives, I was game to try.

Presently a shot rang out from a distance of about 300 yards. It sounded like it came from the direction of an elderly gentleman who was experiencing his first elk hunt. Two more shots followed, and I heard a series of shouts.

Thinking something was amiss, I hurried over and saw the hunter staring down at the ground and dancing around.

"I got a *big* one!" he yelled when he saw me. "It's a real beauty!"

I was excited for the man and ran the rest of the way over, curious about his prize. I looked down to see a bull lying in the brush. It was a four-pointer with a rather small rack, and I immediately slapped the hunter on the back and started taking pictures of him and his elk. Though I expected to see the Bull of the Woods on the ground, I completely understood this hunter's reason for being excited.

"You've got a great elk here," I said to him. "It's a dandy." And it *was* a dandy for that hunter. He was overjoyed, and he had every right to be. That elk would be a trophy as long as the man lived.

But for an avid trophy hunter, the four-point bull would have been quickly passed up. It just didn't come close to the standards set for a trophy-class animal.

And just what are those standards? The official requirements have been set by the Boone and Crockett Club, which is recognized by most hunters as the final word in North American big game trophies. According to B&C, an elk must have a minimum score of 375 points if it's in the American elk category, or 290 if it's the Roosevelt's elk subspecies.

How tough is it to kill an elk big enough to make the record book? Darned tough, if you consider these statistics: About 100,000 elk are killed in the West each year, of which less than a dozen will make the prestigious book!

The big question, of course, is *where* to go to get a look at one of these behemoths. Obviously, the record book is a good place to start your research. By checking the listings, you can determine where most of the record heads are coming from. Keep in mind, however, that times change, and so do elk hunting and elk management. Areas that produced big elk 10 or 20 years ago might not be worth hunting now.

This is the world-record Rocky Mountain bull elk as listed in the Boone and Crockett book. It was killed by John Plute in Dark Canyon, Colorado in 1899 and scores 442 3/8.

Let's examine the eighth and most recent edition of the book. You'll notice that Roosevelt's elk are not listed in the book. This subspecies was recently awarded individual status and is now listed separately. However, a new B&C Book,

William H. Nesbitt, Administrative Director of the Boone and
Crockett Club, shows the world record Roosevelt elk as Nesbitt
was dismantling exhibits after the Boone and Crockett Banquet
and Awards Ceremony in Dallas. The bull scores 356 and was
killed by Pravomil L. Raichl in Oregon in 1959.

18th Big Game Awards, was published in 1984 and lists new
records entered between 1980 and 1982. Roosevelt's elk are
included, with 44 heads listed. Of those, 31 were killed in
Oregon, nine in Washington, three in British Columbia, and
one in California.

State or Province	Number of Record Heads
Montana	61
Wyoming	42
Alberta	29
Colorado	27
Idaho	25

Arizona	18
Oregon	6
New Mexico	4
Saskatchewan	4
Manitoba	3
Washington	2
Texas	1
Unknown	6
Total	228

Those totals are all-time records. Let's see where recent trophy heads are coming from. The following list shows the breakdown since 1975:

Montana	6
Arizona	4
Alberta	3
Idaho	3
Wyoming	2
Total	18

Montana comes out on top both times. Let's take a look at this state, which, incidentally, is the biggest in the Rockies. Despite its size, however, less than half of Montana is elk range. Most of the prime elk country is in the western half. There you'll find many national forests and heavily timbered lands perfectly suited to elk. Big bulls dwell everywhere, though the southwest region is probably home to the most trophy-class elk.

It's no secret that some of the biggest bulls have come from the region just outside Yellowstone Park. Bulls are protected in the park, and only those that leave and enter hunting units are fair game. Special migration hunts account for plenty of huge bulls being taken. To get in on a migration hunt, you must be lucky enough to win a tag in a lottery drawing. The computer selects your hunting dates, which are of two or four days duration, depending on the period you draw.

Other than the late hunt, you can kill the bull of your dreams by hunting public land in Montana. All you need do is find him, and rest assured he'll be in a nightmare jungle where no other human being cares to tread. Of course, you might get lucky and stumble into him, but that eventuality is most unlikely. You'll need to work hard for your trophy elk, probably harder than you've ever worked on a hunt before.

Of the other states and provinces listed, Arizona and New Mexico deserve special mention. These are the states with the best odds of tipping over a Boone and Crockett elk. Be aware, however, that you might have to spend a bit of money and perhaps place your name on a waiting list before centering your crosshairs on your dream Elk.

Both states have a number of Indian reservations and large, private ranches that hold big elk—monster animals that are candidates for the record book. With some perseverance and luck, your best chances for a B&C elk are in the Southwest. As I mentioned, you might have to part with a substantial amount of cash to see your big elk. I know of one Indian tribe that charges $7,000 for a hunt, and more than 500 hunters are on their waiting list. The price is expected to rise substantially in the near future.

That's not to say, however, that you can't tie your tag to a *muy grande* bull in other states. Wyoming has some excellent places to hunt, and Idaho has some superb bulls as well. And don't overlook Canada. Alberta has some immense bulls, and British Columbia and Manitoba have some lovely bulls roaming their forests.

If you're an astute trophy elk hunter, you'll note that Colorado does not have a single elk in the book since 1975. That's ironic, because the biggest elk in the world was taken in Colorado in 1899. That wonderful beast was killed by John Plute in a place aptly named Dark Canyon. The rack garnered a whopping score of 442 3/8, and is located in the

This is not quite a trophy by Boone and Crockett standards but is nonetheless a superb bull taken in Montana, the state that has produced more trophy elk than any other.

lovely town of Crested Butte, Colorado. If you want to see this trophy, don't expect to see billboards and signs pointing to its location. You'll find the elk in a quaint little hardware store in the middle of town. If you go in the winter, you'll likely see a local elderly man or two hunkered over the woodstove, spitting tobacco juice in the general direction of the spittoon. The elk is positioned on the wall near the white-gas containers, and a very small sign that is hard to read interprets the bull's notoriety. If you're an avid elk hunter, you owe it to yourself to see this gorgeous mount.

There are reasons why Colorado is absent from the book since 1975. Incidentally, this state is tops in elk populations, number of elk hunters, and numbers of elk harvested annually. Colorado allows unlimited numbers of hunters to pursue elk, and that management plan is designed to harvest

If you're ever in Crested Butte, Colorado and want to see the world record elk, take a stroll into this store. The bull is owned by Ed Rozman.

quantity rather than quality. In some units, there are as few as three bulls for every 100 elk, and spikes make up the majority of the bull harvest. Killing a really big six-point bull in Colorado is cause for celebration.

But there is hope. Several new limited-entry units have been established in prime elk country, and I'm expecting some huge bulls to be the result. To hunt these units, you'll need to draw a tag in a lottery.If you're a trophy hunter, this endeavor will be worth your while. I predict Colorado will start producing Boone and Crockett heads by the year 1987, if not before. I intend to try for one of those super bulls myself.

If your heart is set on a trophy elk, do yourself a favor and learn how to judge antlers. That won't be easy, because a mature bull sports a big rack. You'll have to be cool, calm, and collected when you stare at that headgear through bin-

This is a long sought-after bull, one many hunters would love to take. Look closely and you'll see 7 points on each side.

oculars or riflescope and make the decision that will ultimately cause your trigger finger to tighten and send a bullet off into him.

When you evaluate a bull, your initial instincts will basically guide you. If he's a really big animal, you won't need to do much looking to decide what to do. But if you're fortunate and are able to closely look over many big bulls, you'll need some standard of reference.

The royal, or fourth, tine is a good indication of a bull's worth. If the tine appears to be 20 inches in length, you're looking at a nice bull. If the other tines have good length and mass, and the antlers are symmetrical, think hard about passing up this big boy. The length of the main beams are important too, but they're hard to judge. A trophy bull will have beams at least 50 inches long.

Every now and then I hear about bulls that have beams so long they'd "scratch the bull's fanny." I'd like to see one of

What have we here? A rare nontypical rack? Look again. Zumbo captured this pair of bulls on film as they bedded close together.

those elk, and I rather suspect the observers have been hallucinating or are otherwise subject to prevaricating in the worst degree.

A hunt on the famed Vermejo Park in New Mexico made me realize just how hard it is to judge a living, breathing bull. On opening morning I was ready to zap a superb elk, but my guide told me to let him go, figuring we could do much better. I followed instructions, and for the next several days I learned how to restrain my trigger finger as bull after bull waltzed across my scope's field of view. Finally I slipped a Nosler bullet into the rib cage of a lovely seven-point elk, forever grateful that I heeded my guide's advice. It was a frustrating experience, but it paid off in the long run.

There are times when your chances of looking a big bull eye to eye are much better than during other periods of the year. As you'll read elsewhere in this book, the bugling season in September and early October are prime times because breeding elk lose much of their natural wariness. Late season is a fine period as well, because big bulls commonly band together and evict the high country as snow pushes them down to lower elevations.

As I mentioned in this chapter, Colorado has limited-entry hunts where you must draw for a tag. Other states have limited hunts, all of which are worth the bother of applying for. Because hunter pressure is reduced, you'll have minimal competition from other hunters. Most importantly, the restrictive permits allow elk to grow older and grow big antlers.

When you hunt a trophy bull, remember that you're dealing with an animal that has escaped hunters for a half-dozen years or more. Hunter pressure being what it is, there aren't many places in the West where elk can live that long, especially on public land. That's enough reason to have the utmost respect for the quarry. Don't expect him to be an

Jim Zumbo capes a bull's head. Don't do this unless you have some experience, or you can ruin the cape.

OFFICIAL SCORING SYSTEM FOR NORTH AMERICAN BIG GAME TROPHIES

Records of North American Big Game	BOONE AND CROCKETT CLUB	205 South Patrick Street Alexandria, Virginia 22314

Minimum Score:
Roosevelt 290
American 375

WAPITI   Kind of Wapiti _____

DETAIL OF POINT MEASUREMENT

	Abnormal Points	
	Right	Left
	Total to E	

SEE OTHER SIDE FOR INSTRUCTIONS			Column 1	Column 2	Column 3	Column 4
	R.	L.	Spread Credit	Right Antler	Left Antler	Difference
A. Number of Points on Each Antler						
B. Tip to Tip Spread						
C. Greatest Spread						
D. Inside Spread of Main Beams	Credit may equal but not exceed length of longer antler					
IF Spread exceeds longer antler, enter difference.						
E. Total of Lengths of all Abnormal Points						
F. Length of Main Beam						
G-1. Length of First Point						
G-2. Length of Second Point						
G-3. Length of Third Point						
G-4. Length of Fourth (Royal) Point						
G-5. Length of Fifth Point						
G-6. Length of Sixth Point, if present						
G-7. Length of Seventh Point, if present						
H-1. Circumference at Smallest Place Between First and Second Points						
H-2. Circumference at Smallest Place Between Second and Third Points						
H-3. Circumference at Smallest Place Between Third and Fourth Points						
H-4. Circumference at Smallest Place Between Fourth and Fifth Points						
TOTALS						

ADD	Column 1		Exact locality where killed
	Column 2		Date killed By whom killed
	Column 3		Present owner
	Total		Address
SUBTRACT Column 4			Guide's Name and Address
FINAL SCORE			Remarks: (Mention any abnormalities or unique qualities)

easy quarry, because he probably won't, though there are exceptions.

I recall a huge bull killed on the Vermejo Park the same day I killed my seven-pointer. It was taken by the late Slim Pickens, the wonderful movie celebrity who loved to hunt.

I certify that I have measured the above trophy on _____ 19____
at (address) _____ City _____ State _____
and that these measurements and data are, to the best of my knowledge and belief, made in accordance
with the instructions given.
Witness: _____ Signature: _____
OFFICIAL MEASURER

INSTRUCTIONS FOR MEASURING WAPITI

All measurements must be made with a ¼-inch flexible steel tape to the nearest one-eighth of an inch.
wherever it is necessary to change direction of measurement, mark a control point and swing tape at
this point. Enter fractional figures in eighths, without reduction. Official measurements cannot
be taken for at least sixty days after the animal was killed.

A. Number of Points on Each Antler. To be counted a point, a projection must be at least one inch
long and its length must exceed the width of its base. All points are measured from tip of point to
nearest edge of beam as illustrated. Beam tip is counted a point but not measured as a point.

B. Tip to Tip Spread is measured between tips of main beams.

C. Greatest Spread is measured between perpendiculars at a right angle to the center line of the
skull at widest part whether across main beams or points.

D. Inside Spread of Main Beams is measured at a right angle to the center line of the skull at widest point between main beams. Enter this measurement again in Spread Credit column if it is less
than or equal to the length of longer antler; if longer, enter longer antler length for Spread Credit.

E. Total of Lengths of all Abnormal Points. Abnormal points are those nontypical in location (such
as points originating from a point or from bottom or sides of main beam) or pattern (extra points,
not generally paired). Measure in usual manner and enter in appropriate blanks.

F. Length of Main Beam is measured from lowest outside edge of burr over outer curve to the most distant point of what is, or appears to be, the main beam. The point of beginning is that point on the
burr where the center line along the outer curve of the beam intersects the burr, then following generally the line of the illustration.

G-1-2-3-4-5-6-7. Length of Normal Points. Normal points project from the top or front of the main
beam in the general pattern illustrated. They are measured from nearest edge of main beam over outer
curve to tip. Lay the tape along the outer curve of the beam so that the top edge of the tape coincides with the top edge of the beam on both sides of the point to determine the baseline for point
measurement. Record point length in appropriate blanks.

H-1-2-3-4. Circumferences are taken as detailed for each measurement.

* * * * * * * * * * * *

FAIR CHASE STATEMENT FOR ALL HUNTER-TAKEN TROPHIES
To make use of the following methods shall be deemed as UNFAIR CHASE and unsportsmanlike, and any
trophy obtained by use of such means is disqualified from entry for Awards.
    I. Spotting or herding game from the air, followed by landing in its vicinity
        for pursuit;
   II. Herding or pursuing game with motor-powered vehicles;
  III. Use of electronic communications for attracting, locating or observing
        game, or guiding the hunter to such game;
   IV. Hunting game confined by artificial barriers, including escape-proof fencing;
        or hunting game transplanted solely for the purpose of commercial shooting.
****
I certify that the trophy scored on this chart was not taken in UNFAIR CHASE as defined above by the
Boone and Crockett Club. I further certify that it was taken in full compliance with local game laws
of the state, province, or territory.
Date _____ Signature of Hunter _____
(Have signature notarized by a Notary Public)

kett Club
ress, written consent)

Official scoring system chart for elk. Courtesy of the Boone and Crockett Club.

When Slim's guide called the bull in with a bugle, the elk dashed straight in without hesitation. Slim claimed it with a superb shot. The bull scored better than 375, but I understand it has never been officially scored.

If you kill a big bull that you suspect will make the record book, make sure it's in a secured area during the required "drying period." A rack that big could attract attention from unscrupulous humans who would eagerly carry it off.

For specific information on measuring the rack, contact the Boone and Crockett Club, 205 South Patrick St., Alexandria, VA 22314.

Hunting a trophy elk requires dedication, stamina, and a special enthusiasm that most hunters lack. You might get lucky and kill a record-class bull, but chances are that you'll need to earn it. Few of those truly giant elk come easy.

CHAPTER 11

Spike Bulls

The bull elk challenged me when I bugled toward the forested basin. I sat quietly in the little clump of trees I'd selected for a stand, and waited for him to make the next move. When he remained silent for five more minutes, I blew into the mouth call again. The elk answered immediately, and this time he was much closer.

A few moments later I spotted movement in the thick spruces. I glassed the area with my binoculars and saw the sight I had hoped for. A cream-colored animal with chocolate mane was slowly moving toward me.

I flipped off the safety, rested my .30/06 solidly on a branch, and found the elk in the scope. I nudged the crosshairs toward his head and found what I was looking for. It was a bull.

This time the crosshairs found the chest area where his lungs were working. When I squeezed the trigger, the elk dashed wildly into the timber, but I knew he was mine. I walked over and found him dead about 10 yards from where he had stood when I fired. It was a fine spike bull.

This is the scenario that occurs tens of thousands of

129

Spikes will weigh 350 to 400 pounds or more. They're considered to be the best eating of all big game.

times each year. But this interesting aspect of elk hunting is unknown to hunters who don't live in elk country, perhaps because all they know about the subject is what they read in outdoor magazines. And outdoor writers generally relate stories only of lovely bulls, magnificent five- and six-point animals that weigh upwards of half a ton.

What most outdoor writers don't tell you is that fewer than 10 percent of the elk killed in the United States are mature trophy bulls. The rest are cows, calves, "rag horns" or small three- or four-pointers, and spikes. Of all the bulls killed in the country each year, 50 to 70 percent are spikes.

Westerners and nonwesterners who hunt elk a great deal will generally kill the first spike that walks by. Why? Because they know the chances of seeing a big bull are slim in most regions. In most hunting circles, any bull is a good bull. Furthermore, a spike bull is perhaps the best eating of any big game animal. His flesh is so similar to grain-fed beef that I take pleasure in fooling friends who would never knowingly eat deer or elk meat. I never tell them afterward that they've eaten part of a spike elk, either. Ignorance is bliss.

To be sure, a spike bull has none of the sagacity and caution of an adult bull who has avoided hunters for three or more years. The yearling bull is unwise to the ways of man and quite vulnerable to hunters. Because spikes usually remain with their family unit through their second winter, they use the old cows as protectors. No doubt their dependence on mama keeps many of them out of trouble and alive. Cows are the eyes and ears of the herd and are the leaders when danger threatens. Indeed, an old cow leads the herds during migrations as well as in escape from enemies. The big bull is usually the last in line.

When breeding season arrives, spike bulls are seen as competitors in the herd by big bulls. Though they've been part of a family unit with cows and calves since they were born, now they must leave temporarily. Mature bulls chase them out of the herds, but spikes often run off a short distance and keep just far enough away to keep the herd bull happy. Spikes are sexually mature, and some observers feel they actually do much of the breeding when the herd bull is off challenging a competitor. Then the spike moves in quickly and breeds a cow.

When a spike is split off from the rest of the herd, he is suddenly on his own. In September when most young bulls are driven from the cows, they are about 18 to 20 months old. This is the time bugling season occurs, and spikes will respond to a proper call made by a hunter. This is not to say a spike bull is a foolish animal. He lacks the instincts of older bulls but has learned much from his mother. Any careless move on the part of the hunter will put a spike to flight instantly.

Almost every bull elk begins his adulthood as a spike, although a few young bulls have forks on one or both sides

A spike often remains with cows and calves as a family unit until a bull kicks him out during the rut.

while others have three or four small points. But it's safe to say that the single spikes are the starting antlers for 90 percent of the bulls that are yearlings.

The term *spike* is a bit misleading, because the antler isn't straight but curved. Studies of thousands of spikes indicate the antlers can be anywhere from 10 to 24 inches long. Generally, the spike antler retains its velvet sheath until the antler drops off in late winter or early spring.

On occasion spike bulls will be allowed to remain in the harem of cows by the big herd bull, perhaps because the larger bull sees the spikes as no threat.

Several years ago, my wife Lois drew a coveted bull permit in a special unit where only 30 tags were authorized. The unit was unique in that much of it was open, and elk were not inhabitants of thickly timbered forests as they usually are elsewhere. Most herds in the unit grazed and bedded in small sagebrush flats surrounded by fairly open junipers.

This spike bull still has velvet on his antlers though the photo was taken late in the fall. This is common among spike bulls.

While Lois and our son, Danny, eased through the junipers along the base of a mountain, I worked my way above them on the mountainside to look for elk ahead. The strategy was to slip up on bedded elk, but if I saw them first I'd back off and hustle down to Lois, then we'd figure a way to get up on them.

I hadn't walked 10 minutes when I saw a dandy herd of elk about 30 strong. I glassed three or four spike bulls and was about to slip down the slope when I saw an antler projecting from behind a juniper. I looked again and made out a beautiful herd bull, a fine six-pointer. He was right in the midst of the cows; the spikes were lying around the perimeter. I started down to join up with Lois when I realized the elk were getting nervous. Several cows got to their feet and stared toward the direction Lois and Danny were approaching. I knew immediately that they were close to the elk, and I did not have time to warn them. They'd no doubt blunder into the herd and Lois might fail to get a shot.

I watched with frustration as the entire herd raised up, testing the air and milling about. The herd bull walked out from under the tree and joined the elk in the opening. Suddenly I heard Lois shoot. I watched the herd from my vantage point, but the big bull gave no sign of being hit. Suddenly a nearby spike flopped down to the ground and kicked its last. It dawned on me that the spike was the object of Lois's attention, either purposely or accidentally. Perhaps she didn't see the herd bull.

The elk herd ran off through the sparse junipers. For five minutes I watched them tear across the flat, with the big bull bringing up the rear. If only I had a permit too, I anguished.

I trotted down to the dead spike. Lois and Danny were already there, grinning when I arrived.

"Didn't you see the herd bull?" I stammered. "He was a beauty. Six points to the side."

"What do I want with a tough old bull?" Lois answered. "I was after something to eat, not a head for the wall."

And that was that. While I field-dressed the spike, I was happy about her choice. I thought about the culinary delights the spike would offer, and I was anxious to age and cut up the carcass for those first tender steaks.

Spike bulls are more numerous than mature bulls for obvious reasons. During its first autumn, the male elk is a calf without antlers, and its chances of surviving the first hunting season are excellent.

A few hunters take calves during antlerless or either-sex seasons, but most settle for a big dry cow. The next year, those surviving males with their new antlers are suddenly legal quarry in areas that allow any bulls to be harvested. Thus, a new generation of bulls are available to hunters.

Many states have enacted regulations protecting spikes in an effort to produce older bulls in the herds. In most cases those experiments have not been as successful as biologists had hoped. Because spikes were protected, there was more pressure on mature bulls, and hunters were afield longer to

Lois Zumbo, author's wife, is proud of this spike she took in Utah. She believes, as do many other hunters, that any bull is a good bull.

Some states exclude spikes from the bull harvest in certain areas and allow various minimum-sized antlers, depending on the regulations. In some states this bull would be considered legal in units where spikes are excluded.

find the warier bulls. In some instances, spikes were shot accidentally and left behind, or shot on purpose and smuggled out of the woods. Most states these days allow "any bull" to be taken, though a few still require a legal bull to have branched antlers.

Since spike bulls hang out with cows and calves whenever they can, they're more vulnerable to hunters, simply because it's easier for hunters to locate an elk herd than a lone bull. Tracks are easier to find and follow, a herd is more visible, and a group of elk often makes plenty of noise. Cows and calves normally squeal and bark at each other when feeding or traveling leisurely through the woods.

Once, when I was hunting elk in Montana, I heard the telltale noises of an elk herd across the canyon I was watching. I glassed the timber and saw a group of elk moving from the trees into a long meadow. No herd bull was present, but two spikes were in the midst of the cows and calves. I left my vantage point, made a stalk across to the elk, and killed a fat spike with 20-inch-long antlers. I might not have seen the elk at all were it not for the noises they made, since I had intended to leave the area about the same time I heard them.

If the wind is right and the woods are reasonably quiet, it's possible to stalk into shooting range of a herd of bedded elk. If it's breeding time, the herd bull might be right in with the cows and calves; otherwise a spike could be in the vicinity.

In areas that are heavily hunted and cover is sparse, opening-day hunters get the pick of the elk and quickly harvest the spikes. This is a good reason to be ready for the opener unless your heart is set on a mature bull. But if it's a "meat" bull you want, locate the elk herd as fast as you can and pick out the spike, if one is available.

Some states offer early and late hunts for elk. In Colorado, for example, there is an early elk hunt in October and a combined elk/deer hunt in early November. I hunted the combined hunt recently and had to work as hard as ever to find a bull, though several small herds of elk were evident. But, because of heavy hunting pressure during the earlier season, I strongly suspected the spikes had been thinned from most herds.

In the event that you're hunting in the snow, tracks are obvious and you have the advantage of determining how fresh they are. Mixed with other elk tracks, a spike bull's print isn't easily identified. Small cows and big calves could be mistaken for a spike's track. But if you spot a set of medium-sized tracks by themselves, chances are good that you're looking at prints made by a spike. Cows seldom travel alone, since they're accompanied by calves or other cows. If a big bull is traveling alone, you can tell by the size of his track. But a loner spike can often be identified by his tracks because other elk seldom travel alone, at least elk that own feet the size that a spike bull does.

During bugling season, a lone spike might answer a call out of curiosity. He won't be looking for a fight, but he'll be interested in the new bull in the territory. Spikes don't bugle with the same intensity and pitch that a mature bull does. At best they cut loose with a high-pitched squeal.

Bowhunters often get a good crack at spikes because bow seasons are often earlier than rifle seasons, and spikes have just been kicked out of the herds by bigger bulls. A friend of mine takes a spike bull almost every year with an arrow by capitalizing on that knowledge. He lures lonely spikes into bow range by bugling in areas where several herds traditionally live.

Generally speaking, cows, calves, and spikes inhabit lower elevations than adult bulls do. This is not a rule but a personal observation. For example, I can hunt elk seven miles from my front door. That means foothill areas blanketed with pinyons, junipers, and pockets of quaking aspens. But the elk I'll find will be small herds of cows, calves, and spikes. The bigger bulls will be in the rough lodgepole pine and alpine fir timber farther up the mountain. Spike bulls

Is this hunter complaining about this one-horned spike bull he took in Utah? Not at all. Look at the smile on the man's face!

won't necessarily be easy to find and kill, but at least they'll be available.

Every year I visit a place close to my house that I know a few elk inhabit. They bed in a thick clump of junipers on a sidehill, and every year I usually find them in the same place. I've never seen more than five elk in the herd, and they're usually cows and calves, but every once in a while a spike shows up. When he does, I'm ready. And doggoned satisfied when I score.

Though he's a yearling, a spike bull will weigh 250 to 400 pounds field-dressed. A suitable firearm is one that will anchor a big mule deer or whitetail, but the elk hunter never knows if he's going to send a bullet into a spike or his granddaddy.

The spike bull will never be a celebrity in the woods, and few writers will write about him. But he's present everywhere there are elk, and though few hunters will grace the wall with his head, he's not to be looked down upon. The trophy hunter will pass him up, hardly giving him a second glance, but to the great majority of hunters, the spike is an honorable quarry, a "meat bull." He's not the Bull of the Woods, but he's still bigger than any mule deer or whitetail you've ever shot. Unless I'm after a trophy, I'll draw down on a spike whenever I can, and so will most other elk hunters. He's a fine game animal, one to be respected. If you doubt my word, head for the Rockies and try elk hunting. And don't be surprised if you kill a spike bull and smile all the way home.

CHAPTER 12

Big Bulls of the Southwest

As every astute elk hunter knows, Arizona and New Mexico have been producing enormous bulls these days. By far the majority of them are being taken from less than a dozen large ranches and Indian reservations.

This chapter addresses the major entities offering trophy elk hunts in the West and describes the type of hunt you might expect. It's impossible to evaluate the hunt program for each by a telephone interview, so I'd suggest you contact the areas you're interested in and ask for several references. Don't be surprised, however, if your request for references is taken as somewhat of an insult by some of the hunt managers. Many of them have waiting lists so long that they could care less about the extra effort and trouble of supplying references.

Fees are usually much higher than they are for elk hunts in other parts of the West, but stop to consider what you're getting before you make any judgments. A standard pack-in outfitted hunt in the Rockies is running about $2500 to $3000 or more for a seven- to 10-day trip. Your chances of killing a trophy bull that scores better than 300

Contrary to popular belief, not all elk are killed near vehicles on southwest ranches. This fine bull is being transported out of the timber by a Vermejo guide.

B&C points are not good on many of those hunts, though some outfitters offer a much better opportunity than others. I'm not downgrading the outfitted horseback hunt—they offer a quality experience in the backcountry, and they certainly fit in the scheme of elk hunting. To be sure, I've enjoyed many wonderful backcountry outings with outfitters, many of whom have become close friends. And I intend to continue those hunts.

What the trophy ranch or reservation offers is an excellent opportunity for a big bull, and often much less strain on the heart, lungs, and leg muscles.

These southwest elk are not tame. With tongue in cheek, I define them as semi-wild.

I offer three definitions of elk. The *tame* elk is one that lives in a fenced enclosure. The hunt generally lasts one day and is fully guaranteed. You pick the bull you want and knock him down. Not much effort or challenge is required.

Jim Zumbo with a good bull he took at Vermejo Park in 1981. The bull scored 333 Boone and Crockett, and to say the author was delighted would be an understatement.

The other end of the spectrum is the *wild-wild* elk. This is a mature bull who lives on a national forest where there is good public access and hunting pressure is heavy. You'll be hard put to find this bull, with hunting success running 15 percent or less.

The *semi-wild* elk dwells in a place where populations are high and hunting is restricted. There are no fences, and big bulls are commonly seen throughout the hunt. They're wary animals, but because of their numbers and light hunting pressure, you have an excellent opportunity to kill a trophy.

Let me describe a southwest hunt I experienced at Vermejo Park. On opening day, my guide Jim Baker and I hiked up a trail that wound through lovely meadows edged by blue spruces and golden aspens. Before daybreak we heard no

Zumbo tosses his hat into the air when he realizes how good his Vermejo bull is. Giant elk make people do strange things.

less than a dozen bulls bugling around us. At shooting light I centered my scope's crosshairs on a very big six-point bull, but Jim told me to let him go. I was astounded. This was the biggest elk I'd seen after more than a dozen years of hunting elk in the Rockies. I followed instructions, and three days later tied my tag to a grand seven-point bull that scored 333 Boone and Crockett points. During that hunt I looked at several dozen bulls that topped 275 B&C, and many of them were better than 300. It was during this same hunt that Slim Pickens killed his gorgeous elk that scored at least 375 B&C points.

The Vermejo accommodates its guests in comfortable lodges amidst a high-country setting. You'll hear coyotes howling and elk bugling as you snuggle in a warm bed with clean sheets. Food is superb, as is the camaraderie.

That's about what you can expect on a southwest trophy elk hunt. You can generally pick your mode of hunting. Whether your style is via vehicle, horseback, or afoot, you can be accommodated. Some areas allow you to hunt without a guide, and on some reservations the fee includes only the permit. You work out the guide fee privately. On some areas you stay in a lodge, in others you overnight in a motel, and in still others you camp on the property in your own unit. Almost all of the ranches and reservations are booked well in advance of the hunt, some as many as three or four years. Write or call for information as soon as you decide to try a hunt.

Here are New Mexico's finest options:

Chama Land and Cattle, P.O. Box 746, Chama, NM 87520 (505/756-2133). This hunt is held on 32,000 acres and offers several five-day hunts and a couple four-day hunts. About 90 percent of the hunters will kill six-point bulls; the other 10 percent will kill five-point bulls. The total hunter success runs at about 100 percent annually.

Jicarilla Apache Indian Reservation, P.O. Box 546, Dulce, NM 87528 (505/759-3255). This 800,000-acre reservation is well known for big mule deer, many of which made the Boone and Crockett book in the early 1960's, but the tribe also offers a quality elk program as well. The tribe offers a five-day hunt that does not include guide service or any accommodations. You stay in a motel in the town of Dulce and make an arrangement with a guide as to his fees, which usually run $100 to $200 or more daily.

Mescalero Apache Indian Reservation, Conservation Department, P.O. Box 176, Mescalero, NM 88340 (505/671-4427). There is usually a waiting list to hunt this reservation. Licenses are available in the spring (usually April or May) on a first-come first-served basis. There are two hunts offered. The package plan includes a one-on-one guide, all services and lodging at the Inn of the Mountain Gods. Breakfast and lunch are provided, but evening dinner is not. The other hunt includes only the tribal permit. You make arrangements with a guide on your own.

Moreno Ranch, P.O. Box 135, Eagle Nest, NM 87718 (505/377-6581). This 50,000-acre ranch usually offers four five-day hunts in October and two in December. All accommodations are provided, with one guide for three hunters. Success is around 90 percent overall, with 75 percent of the bulls being at least five-pointers.

North Country Outfitters, Mountain Route, Box 20, Jemez Springs, NM 87025 (505/829-3897 or -3755). Ric Martin offers four five-day hunts in October on 100,000 acres of land. About 50 guests hunt the property annually, with a hunter success rate of about 85 percent each year. Bulls are in the 280 to 320 B&C class, but several in the 340 to 350 and better range are taken as well. Hunts book very early on this popular ranch. Special archery hunts are offered in September.

Three Rocks Ranch, Box 37, Amarilla Tierra, NM 87575 (505/588-7221). You'll hunt 200,000 acres of private land here, and a number of big bulls in the 6X6 class are shot each season. All accommodations are provided, including license, meat processing, taxidermy fees, and meals at the ranch lodge. The all-inclusive price offers one guide per two hunters.

UU Bar Ranch, Rt. 1, Box 42, Cimarron, NM 87714 (505/376-2643). This ranch offers hunting for big bulls on 120,000 acres. There are usually three five-day trophy hunts annually, and they are booked early. Hunter success is 90 percent for trophy elk. Several B&C bulls were killed over the last several years. Each season, 24 hunters are accommodated, eight per five-day hunt.

Vermejo Park, P.O. Drawer E, Raton, NM 87740 (505/445-3097). This popular ranch offers trophy elk hunting on 400,000 acres. There has been some confusion since Vermejo owners donated 100,000 acres to the U.S. Forest Service recently. There is still excellent elk hunting on the property, with much of the prime elk habitat retained. Bulls in the 300 B&C class are common here, and hunts commonly book a full two years in advance.

Arizona offers three trophy elk hunts on Indian reservations. They include:

Fort Apache Indian Reservation (also called White Mountain Indian Reservation), P.O. Box 220, White Mountain Apache Tribe, Game and Fish Department, White River, AZ 85941 (602/338-4385). According to tribal officials, this is the place for monster bulls. I was told that hunters kill only B&C class bulls, with many ranging 385 and better. During a recent season, two were killed that scored higher than 404 B&C. The hunt begins in late September, and there is a several-year waiting list.

Hualapai Indian Reservation, Box 216, Peach Springs, AZ 86434 (602/769-2227). This reservation is located near the Grand Canyon and offers a September and late November hunt, with 12 persons per hunt. An application must be sent in, and a lottery draw determines winners. The lottery deadline varies; contact the tribe for information. You can camp on the reservation and do the hunt on your own, or hire a guide and make private arrangements. There are some very big bulls on this reservation.

San Carlos Indian Reservation, Box 97, San Carlos, AZ 85550 (602/475-2361). This 2-million-acre reservation offers a 10-day hunt in December. Two hundred permits are usually sold on a first-come basis. They have not been difficult to obtain. You can camp in remote areas and hunt on your own, or hire a guide. Hunter success is commonly 20 percent or so.

The Deseret Land and Livestock Ranch in Utah offers superb trophy bull hunts on 200,000 acres of land. A dozen or so permits are sold each year for the fully guided hunts. All services are provided for the package fee. Contact Deseret Land and Livestock Ranch, P.O. Box 38, Woodruff, UT 84086 (801/794-2885).

The Southern Ute Indian Reservation in Colorado has two late hunts in November and December. Less than two dozen tags are offered, and you must obtain your tag in a lottery. Contact Southern Ute Tribal Affairs Department, Wildlife Conservation Office, P.O. Box 737, Ignatio, CO 81137 (303/563-4525).

These are the major trophy elk regions in the southern and central Rockies, which is essentially where the trophy elk hunts are located. As this book goes to press, most of the hunts are going for about $5,000, and some are expected to hit five-digit figures in the near future.

Yep, a big old bull elk is worth a lot of money. And I can understand why. He's a majestic beast, and lots of folks will pay considerable fees to hunt him. And rightly so.

CHAPTER 13

A BIG BULL'S SECRET

Big bull elk have a peculiar habit that enables them to save their skin during hunting season each fall. Only a handful of hunters know the habit, but those who do capitalize on it handily each fall. I stumbled onto it several years ago, and this knowledge has helped me enormously over the years. The discovery occurred when I was hunting a seemingly impenetrable forest in late October.

Huge spruce and fir trees were crisscrossed atop each other, piled together like giant matchsticks that had fallen helter-skelter in massive clumps. Heavy undergrowth forced its way through openings in the plethora of wood, adding more confusion to the Wyoming jungle.

I carefully maneuvered my way through the timbered maze, almost convinced that I'd never again see uncluttered land. I realized that I'd made a mistake soon after entering the inhospitable forest. For half an hour I climbed over it and crawled under it, hoping to find a shortcut to a basin below.

I had been elk hunting for five days and, so far, I hadn't seen a good bull. All I'd glimpsed were some cows, calves, and a pair of spike bulls. I knew there were big bulls in the area but I couldn't find one, no matter where I hunted or how hard I tried.

Now, while fighting through the downed timber, all my thoughts and efforts were tuned to getting out of the nightmarish tangle. I made no attempt to be quiet, because I hadn't seen an elk track in the last hour and was convinced that I was miles from the nearest living, breathing elk.

Progress in the timber was slow. Finally, I worked my way to a spot that was not quite as thick. I stopped for a quick rest, and my eye caught sight of a surprising find on the forest floor. A group of fresh elk pellets glistened in the sun.

An elk? In this impervious, pathless thicket? I immediately assumed that the animal that had been here was a cow because no bull could possibly have coaxed antlers through the upended forest, at least not a big bull.

With sudden interest, I took a look around me. I was in somewhat of an oasis in the midst of one of the heaviest blowdowns I'd ever seen. For many years I had worked as a forest ranger. I'd been in horrid jungles around the country, but this was one of the worst.

Instinctively, I slipped along quietly, but if any elk were nearby, they had heard me half an hour before. I had been breaking branches and twigs loudly as I moved through the timber.

I took a few steps and saw another pile of pellets, then another. After a few moments of further investigation, I'd seen several dozen groups of droppings. Obviously, I'd stumbled into a place where a herd of elk had been recently. I was puzzled. The droppings were all the same large size— the kind that would be produced by a single big elk. If a herd of elk had been in the area, droppings would be different sizes because of the various ages of elk in the herd.

After walking 10 yards, I saw a distinct track on the forest floor. I was astounded. There was no question that an enormous elk had made the imprint, and only a bull could grow that big.

I was still staring at the track when an animal crashed through the timber 25 yards away. I looked up to glimpse a great bull elk twisting and weaving in and out of the slanted trees. I quickly put my rifle to my shoulder, but he vanished from sight. I stood helpless and listened for more than a minute as the elk slammed his half-ton body through the forest.

After my nerves settled down, I looked around and estimated that the bull had apparently been living in the area for several weeks. A small creek ran through the timbered spot, and there was heavily grazed grass wherever there was space among the downed logs and underbrush.

I followed the path of the frightened elk and was amazed to see where he'd gotten out of the blowdown. Despite his large antlers, he had managed to break through an impossible mass of jumbled trees and branches.

My hunt ended on a happy note, although I didn't kill a

This is often the only sight you'll see of a bull when you jump him from his nest. Shoot fast, but only if you're sure of a clean hit in the vitals.

big bull. I took a modest four-point elk that was with a herd of cows and calves. I was able to trail the herd after a two-inch snowfall, and I killed the bull in his bed. I never forgot the incident with the big bull, however.

Two years later, I was bear hunting with Billy Stockton. It was early June, and we were watching a big meadow late in the afternoon. Billy had seen bears feeding there often in the spring. We hoped to spot one and stalk it before nightfall.

We were sitting quietly when Billy tapped me lightly on the shoulder. I turned to see him glassing the upper edge of the meadow with binoculars.

"Look at those elk," Billy said. "They're just coming out to feed, and two of them will be real beauties this fall."

I focused my binoculars on the foraging animals and saw what Billy meant. Two of the elk already had massive antlers coated with velvet.

Billy slapped at a mosquito, leaned back against a tree, and tossed a pine cone at nothing in particular.

"Those bulls will be nowhere to be seen during the regular gun season," Billy mused. "They'll be plumb out of sight and almost impossible to find."

"What do you mean?" I asked. "Where do they go?"

"They go to their nests," Billy said simply.

I sat quietly and thought about Billy's statement. I was perplexed. A nest? I'd never heard of such a thing, and I'd been hunting elk in the West for more than 20 years. I was almost ashamed to ask the obvious question.

"What's a nest?" I queried.

"After the rut is over, a big smart bull will head off by himself," Billy explained. "He'll find a place where there's water and grass and stay for up to a month or more. I call the hideout a nest. The bull will hang around in it and never show himself, and he'll practically starve before he comes out. Usually, he'll leave when snow starts to pile deep. Then he'll travel down to winter range and join up with other elk."

I was intrigued and asked Billy how big an elk nest was.

"I've seen them no bigger than a half-acre," Billy responded. "The bull will eat every strand of grass, and the droppings will be so thick you'd think you were in a sheep pen.

"Most of the nests are in unbelievable places," he continued. "I've seen a big bull go into a spot that you and I would have to crawl to reach."

"How do you hunt them?" I asked.

"There's only one way," Billy said. "You go in the heavy timber after them and hope you'll stumble into a nest. Once he's in his hideout, he won't move for anything. You've got to practically walk up to him to get him up on his feet. And you have to be ready. You might get only one quick shot because he'll rip through that timber.

"You'll never see a fresh track until you're right in the nest," Billy added. "It's quite a shock to walk into such a place."

"Do your hunters get many of those big bulls?" I asked.

"Not many," he told me. "Most hunters just won't work that hard. It's all footwork day after day. A hunter has to be in good shape to keep going, and he has to be confident. If his brain gives out, so will his legs. A lot of hunters don't understand. They think we can glass a backcountry meadow early in the morning, find a feeding bull, and put on a stalk. But it doesn't work that way, at least not with big bulls in my country who have been around a few years. They just don't go into meadows.

"The rut season is another story," Billy added. "A big bull's brains go plumb to hell. He's all lathered up, full of love and fight, and he'll do stupid things. He's always on the move, guarding his harem, looking for cows, or chasing off other bulls. He's bugling, grunting, and making all sorts of noise. If you can't bugle him in with a call, you can listen to him whistle and then move in.

"Trouble is," Billy went on, "the Montana gun season

Billy Stockton, a Montana outfitter who hunts bulls in their lairs, packs out a huge elk rack taken by one of his hunters.

starts late in October. The rut is over by then, and the bulls are sulking in their nests. Bowhunters have it a whole lot better, though. The season is in September and early October when bulls are loco. Practically every one of my bowhunters will get a shot at a good bull. But some of the gun hunters leave without seeing a big bull and are convinced that there are no trophy elk in my area. But I know better."

I knew better, too. Some of the biggest bulls in the country have been taken from the forested regions where Billy hunts.

Billy's explanation about elk nests was enlightening and accounted for my incident with the Wyoming bull.

Some time later, I shared a campfire with Jack Atcheson of Butte, Montana, and we discussed elk nests. Jack is a well-known taxidermist and hunter's booking agent. He is also an expert elk hunter.

"The best elk hunter I know refuses to hunt opening week of the season," Jack told me. "Bulls are scattered far and wide and are spooked constantly by hunters. He waits until bulls go to their 'places' and hunts them after they're settled in."

Jack told me about an experience he'd had with an elk in its lair.

"I was hunting near a popular ski area," he said. "And I felt sort of silly because I could hear music and people from the ski slope. I was confident that there was a bull around, though. I'd hunted the area before and knew elk liked it. The mountain was thickly timbered, and I walked for several hours before I came to a dense pocket in the trees. I worked my way in and saw droppings and tracks everywhere. The snow was beat down by the elk, and I knew I was in a hiding spot. I jumped the bull and killed him just as he bounced out of his bed. There was no question that he had been living there for weeks, judging by the sign. The noise from the recreation area didn't bother him because he wasn't disturbed. He felt he was in a safe place."

A nice elk like this spends a lot of time hiding in a lair where he isn't disturbed by hunters. He might spend several weeks in his nest and never leave it.

I had a similar experience with an elk that was content to hide near people. It was the last day of the Utah elk season, and my son Danny had been pestering me to make a final try for a bull. Though our front door is just seven miles from elk country, crowds of hunters had hammered the area every day of the season. Seeing any elk, even a cow, would have been a major accomplishment, and a spike bull was almost beyond question. Danny was too young to hunt, and my heart wasn't really into elk hunting because I had other work to do. So I convinced him that we'd spend the first two hours of shooting light glassing far-off mountain slopes and basins. If that failed, and I knew it would, we'd spend the rest of the morning walking a ridge or two and head home early.

As expected, our glassing efforts were futile. I was driving aimlessly, wondering where to go, when some friends drove up and waved for us to pull over. They had found a spot where some animals had broken the ice on a tiny waterhole to get a drink, but the hunters couldn't stay to check the surrounding area out because they had to be in town soon. They told me where the waterhole was, and Danny and I wasted no time getting there.

I checked the ground carefully around the water and made out the distinct track of an elk in the frost. It was hard to see, but it was there and it was fresh. The elk had watered in the night.

I was amazed. The waterhole was just 75 yards from the road and on the edge of a thick patch of junipers. While we looked for some sign, at least six pickup trucks full of hunters went by.

Checking the wind direction, Danny and I entered the juniper thicket with the breeze in our faces. We hadn't gone 100 yards when we spotted fresh dropping—dozens of piles that were recently deposited. I came to an immediate halt and realized that we'd discovered an elk nest. I was about to tell Danny to sit quietly while I pussyfooted around when I saw an odd color in a thick clump of trees 20 yards ahead.

I raised my binoculars, and the realization that I was looking at an elk quickened my pulse and gave me the shakes. The animal appeared to be bedded, but I couldn't be sure. I could see only parts of its chest, neck, and face. The animal's head was obscured by branches, but I was convinced that I was seeing antlers in the foliage. The elk was staring at me with total concentration, and I could see its unblinking eyes. I desperately tried to see antlers, and I hoped the elk would move its head just a fraction of an inch so I could spot antler movement in the trees. If I saw that, the hunt would be over. I stood with my .30/06 shouldered, my thumb on the safety, ready to fire. But nothing happened other than an unnerving staring match.

Suddenly, the elk leaped to its feet. I saw its giant rack for a split second as the bull burst into the trees. He was gone before I could get the safety off, and his initial bound took him over the crest of a small knoll.

This is the result if you can outsmart a big bull that hides in a thicket for long periods of time.

The elk was gone. I had him dead to rights, but he had outsmarted me. I told no one about the incident afterward because they wouldn't have believed me.

The bull stayed in that nest because he hadn't been bothered by hunters. This was true even though he was hiding within 200 yards of a well-traveled road. He had feed in the trees, and the nearby waterhole was available to satisfy his thirst.

As luck would have it, I wandered into another elk nest in Colorado two weeks later. This time the results were different. A big five-point bull made the mistake of letting me get within 10 yards of him before exploding out of his bed. I knocked him down with a bullet through both lungs.

The concept of big bulls using a nest or lair is contrary to what we normally think about elk movements. Few hunters are aware of this behavior. Most of us figure that elk lay up in the timber during the day and come out to feed in open meadows late in the afternoon, during the night, and early in the morning. To that end, we expend our efforts doing too much glassing and not enough walking.

Walking is the only way to find a giant bull that is holed up. You can ride horseback in a great deal of elk country, but a horse can't go where an elk can. In addition, if an elk bursts out of cover, you need to be on solid ground where you can get a shot, and that's not going to happen atop a horse. A terrified elk won't give you much time, and he won't stop to look back.

The next time you're convinced that elk are long gone from the country you're hunting, try slinking around in the nastiest, most miserable cover you can find. Remember that it doesn't have to be miles back in the hinterlands. You might kill the biggest bull of your life in a surprisingly accessible place.

Keep in mind that you can walk by an elk's lair and miss it by only a few feet. It's a good idea to work a thick patch of timber for elk just as you would a grouse covert or a weedy place where pheasants like to live.

Chances are good that a hiding bull will hear you, because you'll be in heavy cover with plenty of brittle branches. He's apt to stay put and wait you out, though, just as a crafty pheasant will. If you come to a thick spot and you have a hunch that an elk is home, circle until the breeze is blowing toward you from the thicket. You might be able to smell the distinctive odor of an elk. If you do, or if you suddenly spot unusual amounts of droppings or tracks, be ready for imminent action. Your bull is probably glaring at you from the innards of the jungle. Do your part and he'll be yours.

CHAPTER 14

Elk Hunting with the Crowds

Elk hunting is commonly perceived as a backcountry scenario in which the hunter and elk are engaged in a one-on-one affair, and the only sounds to be heard are wild noises of the forest.

If you believe that, then you're in for a rude awakening the first time you try for elk where there is good public access. Consider these statistics: In Colorado, the top elk state in terms of elk populations and annual harvests, hunter success runs only 15 or 20 percent each year. In many units, 75 percent or more of the bull harvest is composed of spikes. Almost 200,000 hunters pursue elk in Colorado each year, and they take about 30,000 animals.

Tagging an elk under those crowded conditions is usually the result of good luck, but there are ways to improve your chances, no matter what state you hunt.

The simplest way is to avoid the crowds in the first place, but that's not always possible. A good option is to hunt during the early season when elk are bugling. To do so you'll have to plan on a backcountry adventure or draw a

160

tag in a lottery. In Montana, Wyoming, and Idaho, a general elk license allows you to hunt early in specific remote areas.

If you don't have a horse and equipment or hire an outfitter, you'll have a big job getting into elk country and bringing an elk carcass back out. Your hunt might turn into an ordeal rather than an enjoyable outing.

Because of the expense of hiring an outfitter and the difficulty of putting together a do-it-yourself elk hunt, hunters often pursue elk from a vehicle. The well-prepared hunters will have a couple of horses tied in base camp to haul elk out; but most hunters will go afoot and hope they kill an elk close enough to a road where they can drive close to it. That's wishful thinking, however, and is usually an exception.

Because of access problems, you'll see few people in the backcountry, and elk hunting will be at its best. Bulls respond to bugle calls as the animals compete for cows. In Idaho and Montana, the nonresident must buy an elk license on a first-come basis; nonresidents who wish to hunt Wyoming must draw a general license tag in a lottery.

Most states offer quality elk hunts that offer limited numbers of elk tags available in a lottery. If you can draw a tag, you'll have limited competition from other hunters because of the restrictive license procedure, and you'll have a fine opportunity to take a big bull. But drawing one of those tags is on a par with hitting a slot machine for a big jackpot in Las Vegas. Odds are tough, but if you obtain a tag you can often find a dandy bull with a minimum of expense and effort. I know some quality areas where you can see elk from a vehicle every day.

The majority of elk hunters will not have it so good, however. In prime elk country you can count on crowds everywhere, and you'll be hard-pressed to drive down a road that doesn't have fresh tire tracks, no matter how rugged it is.

Almost all of the pressure will be in the higher elevations, up in the quaking aspens, pines, firs, and spruces.

Crowds in the elk woods are all too common. Many hunters use horses, and you need to be astute and in good shape to score in view of the tough odds.

That's supposed to be where elk hang out, and in fact, it *is* the preferred habitat for the animals. But that doesn't mean that they'll *stay* there when the shooting starts, which leads up to my first tip.

Let me offer an example. A few years ago, Don Smith was flying over a popular elk area in Utah on opening morning. Smith was director of the Utah Division of Wildlife Resources and was observing the hunt from the air while returning from a wildlife meeting.

"I saw orange-clad figures on every ridge and slope and said to myself that no elk in his right mind would be caught in that circus," Smith remarked. "Then I looked out the other window and saw 60 head of elk running full bore for the badlands. There wasn't a hunter within three miles of the herd. What amazed me was the swift reaction of the elk to the presence of hunters. The season was open only a few hours and the animals wasted no time getting out of there."

The "badlands" Smith referred to is low-elevation pin-yon/juniper forest. It's not uncommon for elk to seek shelter in those forests, but few hunters realize that elk are in them, perhaps because the forests are arid and so unlike traditional elk habitat. This forest type is extensive in the West, covering much of Colorado, Utah, Arizona, and New Mexico. Elk use it regularly, not only for escape cover but also for routine living requirements.

Several years ago I was cutting firewood during elk season in a low elevation juniper forest with my wife and children. I already had my elk and wasn't paying much attention to anything other than the task of sawing wood. My wife suddenly called and asked me to look at tracks in the soil.

"Aren't they elk tracks," she said, "and if so, why are the elk so far from the high country?"

I looked and verified her suspicions. A small herd of elk indeed lived in the area. I put the chainsaw down and inves-tigated further. The tracks led to a small spring where the animals had watered. More tracking showed that they were grazing in a grassy opening on a sidehill where the junipers were thick. I half expected to see elk because fresh sign was everywhere in the forest, but at the same time I was dumb-founded to see them in an environment that could almost be classified as desert.

The following year, I visited the area before elk season. I quickly located fresh sign, convincing me that the animals lived in the area almost year-round and weren't using it just to escape from hunters. I had other commitments that sea-son and didn't hunt, but I returned for three years after-ward. I saw cows and calves on each visit, and during the third season I killed a modest four-point bull. I never saw another hunter during those forays, and I was smugly satis-fied to know that thousands of hunters were looking for elk in the national forest four miles away, and hundreds of them would never see an elk during the entire season.

As I learned more about those lowland elk, I talked to

wildlife officials and avid hunters, and came to the conclusion that elk readily adapt to marginal areas outside their usual high-elevation domains. Some traveled rapidly to those places when disturbed by hunters, as Don Smith witnessed, and some chose to live there for most of the year.

Besides pinyon and juniper forests, elk commonly hide out in thick stands of oak brush, which grows just below quaking aspens in the elevational regime of forest types. If you've ever hunted the scrub oaks of the Rockies, you'll know what it means to fight and crawl through horrid cover. It's hard to imagine that a large animal such as an elk can get through it, but let me assure you they do.

There are other places where elk hide, all of them where people seldom look. That's why the elk are there, because no one bothers them.

Another way to beat the crowds is to bide your time and wait until snow forces elk to leave the higher elevations. The annual migration usually begins in late November and early December, but unexpected storms can start elk moving prematurely. Two factors determine the success of a late hunt: The weather must cooperate, and the state you're hunting must offer a hunt that coincides with migration. Only a few states offer late hunts, and many seasons require a lottery draw for a permit. Two famous late hunts are held outside Yellowstone Park each winter. Seasons run through February, but tags are tough to draw.

Though there are early, late, and limited hunts, the typical hunter will take his chances and hunt during the general season. He'll have plenty of company, and he'll need to compete with other hunters. He might get lucky and score, but he'll have to use ingenuity and common sense to take elk consistently.

The season of the crowds in elk country is also the season when elk are most uncooperative. Not only are they harassed by humans but they're also disinterested in bugle calls and won't respond to a challenge. What's more, the entire forest is available to elk as escape cover, from glacial

This is the standard bull in forests crowded with hunters. In some units, spikes make up more than 75 percent of the bull harvest.

cirques above timberline to thick stands of lodgepole pine and Douglas fir. Snow hasn't driven them out of the high country yet, and elk can hide anywhere.

Unlike deer, which are ubiquitous and can be located wherever there is good cover, elk travel in herds and stay together for much of the year. Finding one band of elk in a forest, even a *good* forest for elk hunting, can be a major undertaking. Each year I talk to dozens of hunters who didn't see an elk during the entire season, and those hunters were in places where elk were fairly common. The country is big and heavily forested, and unless you have some workable strategies you might be hard-pressed to stumble onto an elk.

A few years ago, a friend had hunted for several straight days in a thick lodgepole forest and hadn't seen an elk. Undaunted, he continued his pursuit and walked 10 or 12 miles a day. On the seventh day he spotted a spike bull grazing in a tiny clearing in the midst of heavy timber three miles from the nearest road. He killed the spike, but only by perseverance and determination. The forest he hunted was crowded with hunters, but most of them didn't venture more than a mile from a road, and few were willing to leave well-established trails.

My friend had an important advantage. He didn't fear the forest and wandered into its dark and hidden recesses where few people went.

It's common for hunters unfamiliar with the West to be intimidated by the vastness of its mountainous regions. An eastern hunter admitted to an outfitter friend of mine that he was totally unnerved while hunting in Montana. "It was a great hunt and I had a terrific experience," the hunter told the outfitter, "but I'll never come back. I was scared to death in that country. It was too big, and I was uncomfortable in that remote camp."

The hunter was honest, and his feelings are shared by many others. So the answer is to hunt where surroundings are familiar, or to walk trails and old roads or follow fence-lines and creeks. That's an understandable choice, and I'm not ridiculing hunters who do so, but it's also the best way to stay in the crowds and not see elk.

The key is to get into areas shunned by other hunters, either because they're remote or they just don't "look" like elk country as scrub oak stands or juniper forests. Sometimes elk will descend into deep, sheer-walled canyons and remain holed up until the season is over. I know of such a place, having discovered it while fishing for cutthroats in the summer. Numerous groups of elk droppings tipped me off, and I learned later from a friend that two or three locals hunted it on an irregular basis. They'd taken some big bulls and kept their secret to themselves. I went in once and saw two big six-point bulls but couldn't get a shot. I managed to tie my tag to a five-point elk the following day, however. But the area has since been discovered by hunters because of mining that takes place there, and it is no longer a haven for elk.

To find secluded areas you must be willing to expend some time and energy. If you're a bit nervous in western forests, obtain a good map and study it. Become familiar with the region and look for inaccessible spots on the map. Before you ever see the area, you should have a good idea of major landmarks, water courses, and access roads. When you plan your hunt, allow some time to scout the region, and connect the information you've stored in your head from studying the map with the actual layout of the land.

Scouting is essential if you want good odds of seeing and killing an elk. Keep in mind the fact that when opening day arrives, you're going to be competing fiercely with other hunters, perhaps dozens or even hundreds of them. Whatever you can do to gain an advantage is a plus in your favor, and the smartest thing to do is locate elk before the season opens when they're reasonably undisturbed.

Don't assume that the fact you've found elk will mean that they'll be where you last saw them, however. You can bet that other hunters will be scouting, and the human presence and activity will make elk uneasy. For that reason, try to keep track of a herd right up until the end of daylight on the eve of opening morning. If you can do that the elk will probably be in the general area on the opener, and you'll have an excellent chance of getting one.

Elk hunting statistics in Colorado show just how important it is to hunt hard and sensibly on opening day. The state has two separate 11-day elk seasons each year. Of the total 22 days, by far the most elk are killed on the first day.

In 1982, for example, 28 percent of the yearly harvest was taken opening day. The second day resulted with 12 percent of the total kill, and 8 percent was taken on the third day. Almost half of the harvest came from the first three days.

In 1982, I hunted Colorado with two pals. We hunted a popular area, and we knew we'd be faced with heavy hunter pressure. We scouted hard for two days immediately prior to the season and located two elk herds and several places where fresh sign indicated that they were feeding.

Our hunt was superb. Each of us killed five-point bulls. We took one each on the first, second, and third days of the season, and in every case we had outwitted other hunters in the vicinity. We got up early in the morning and were deep in the forest long before daylight, and we hunted in rugged, steep spots where other hunters refused to go.

Another way to beat the crowds is to be well-prepared with sturdy vehicles and equipment. I don't know how many times I've seen traffic snarls on high-country forest roads because inexperienced hunters tried to drive in full-size motorhomes and vehicles that should never be driven off the pavement. A good vehicle will get you into the hinterlands, and you'll have that much more of an advantage. If it snows, you won't have to panic and hurry out of the high-elevation country.

That's not to say you should ignore storm warnings, however. If you're hunting in mid-November or so and the radio forecasts severe snowstorms expected to last several days, get out of the high country as soon as you can. You might have a harrowing experience, and it might be the following spring before you see your stranded vehicle again. Snow can pile three or four feet deep in the Rockies in a big hurry.

As another bit of advice, be careful about the amount of information you pass on to members of other hunting parties. It might seem downright unfriendly to say this, but keep in mind that every hunter out there is a competitor. Each has a rifle and a tag, and each will try his or her

A bull of this stature is tough to find where crowds are common. Too many hunters keep heavy pressure on elk and crop bulls so consistently that elk don't get a chance to grow old enough to wear large antlers.

utmost to kill an elk before you do. Of course, members of your own party are different. I'm not suggesting you shun hunters and be hostile. Just don't volunteer information that you've worked hard to find, because other hunters might use that knowledge in the spirit of competition and score at your expense. You certainly wouldn't tell a stranger that you found where a herd of elk had been feeding the night before, or that you found a spring where animals are watering.

Sometimes you can reverse this attitude and team up with other parties. If elk are evasive in a thick forest, you can set up a drive with groups of other hunters. Sit around a campfire or in a tent and figure a strategy. Elk can sometimes be driven effectively; the more hunters the better in most cases. Of course, it's every hunter to himself, and even though you're competing with one another, you're still involved in a team effort.

When you hunt with the crowds, two parts of your body are important: your legs and your brain. Use both of them hard, but be sure your heart and lungs are up to the task. Elk hunting is tough, tough work. If you want to be in the enviable minority of hunters who score, plan your elk hunt long before the season begins, and don't give up until the last day of the hunt. You can't kill an elk unless you're out where the elk live. That's my best piece of advice. Remember it.

CHAPTER 15

What You Should Know About Outfitters and Guides

There are three good reasons why you should hire an outfitter: He'll take you into elk country, help you find an elk, and haul it out if you score.

There's another reason. An outfitter will take care of your food and shelter requirements and make you comfortable in the backcountry. If you're tired and miserable from tending to camp chores, you won't hunt well. That's not to say a hunter is incapable of caring for himself. But a trip in a remote area takes a lot of doing, and your chances of scoring will be better if you apply your energies to hunting, which is the primary task at hand.

Finding an outfitter to hire is simple. All you need do is look at the ads in outdoor magazines, pick an outfitter, call him up and book a hunt. Right?

Wrong.

It's more involved than that. You must spend some time finding the correct outfitter. Your hunting needs aren't shared by every other hunter, and each outfitter offers a different hunt program.

Here are various ways to locate and contact outfitters:

Outfitters provide plenty of basic comforts and good camaraderie on elk hunts.

Look at ads in outdoor magazines, write to outfitters associations in various states and obtain lists of members, meet outfitters at sportsmen's shows, or book a hunt through an agent.

When you look at magazine ads, be aware that you're only seeing the highlights of an outfitter's operation. There's no way to tell much about that particular person other than the fact that he's in business and has hunts for various species in a certain area. Shop around a bit before you settle on an outfitter. Write letters to three or four and request brochures. In your letter, ask them what their hunter success rates have been over the last several years. Outfitters often balk at this question, but it's a fair one and you should know the answer.

While on the subject of writing, let me make a point. Do the outfitter a favor and don't write unless you're serious about a hunt. They're businessmen and shouldn't have to bother with people who are just curious and are not interested in booking a hunt. Outfitters tell me this is a pet peeve, and I don't blame them. To put this in perspective, say you owned a store and 20 people walked in every day, took up your valuable time by asking questions, and walked out with no intentions of buying any of your goods. Those people are of no help to you as a businessman, and the same holds true with outfitters. If you're a borderline case and need a little convincing to make a hunt, that's a different story. But if you just want some mail to escape boredom, find another outlet. Outfitters spend a great deal of their time outdoors tending to horses, equipment, and a myriad of other activities. Lots of them aren't fond of sitting down at a desk and writing letters, especially when their efforts are a waste of time.

When you write, ask for references. Obviously, an outfitter is going to send you a list of satisfied clients. That's good business, but it might not be a true indication of his worth. Let's put that in perspective too. Say 10 people are on a hunt and the outfitter is a crook. By luck one of the hunters kills a good elk. The outfitter will send you the name of the happy hunter as a reference, but not the names of the other nine.

There aren't many ways to learn the truth. The best way is to ask for several references. When you get a list, call the hunters instead of writing. You'll get much more information during a phone conversation than you will from a letter.

Before you book a hunt, be absolutely certain you're engaging an outfitter who is properly licensed in the state you're hunting. There are plenty of unscrupulous outfitters out there trying to make a fast buck. As a victim of this thief, you might find yourself in trouble with the law besides having a bad hunt.

Ask the outfitter how many hunters will be teaming up with a guide. One guide per hunter is much more expensive than one guide for every two or three hunters, but your

A well-stocked cook tent is a common sight in an outfitter's camp. The coffee is always on and the meals are great, especially after you've come in after a tough day of hunting.

chances of success are greater. Two people can move faster and more quietly than three or four, and you won't have to flip a coin or outmaneuver your companion to get a shot. One-on-one hunts are fairly rare, however; most outfitters use one guide per two hunters. This is an equitable arrangement. Just be sure the outfitter lives up to his promise.

Don't be shy about querying the outfitters about details of the hunt. Get as much information as you can. Several years ago I hunted with an Idaho outfitter who was supposed to pair two hunters to each guide. It was during the bugling season, and I expected to hunt with calls. It didn't work out that way. Twelve of us rode out of camp on horseback every morning and were positioned around big patches of timber. A couple hours after daybreak, a half-dozen guides walked through the timber to drive elk out. Nothing showed after three days of hunting different areas. Finally I spoke

Cozy, heated tents are provided by outfitters. and camaraderie runs high.

up and told the outfitter I wanted to try hunting alone with my bugle call. He told me the law required that all clients must be accompanied by a guide, and sent me out the next morning with a guide and another hunter. By noon that day we bugled in and killed two good bulls.

These misunderstandings can be avoided by booking a hunt with an agent. Tell him what you want out of the hunt, and he should be able to match you with an outfitter who will accommodate you accordingly. You won't pay extra by booking with an agent. His commission is built into the hunt, just as a travel agent's is.

You can find unscrupulous agents just as you can find shyster outfitters, but they don't last long. Agents who have been around a long time are usually the most reputable, but there are some newcomers to the scene who do a good job as well.

Jack Atcheson, the booking agent out of Butte, Mon-

In wilderness areas, outfitters can't use mechanized tools. Chain saws are forbidden; all wood cutting must be done by hand. This outfitter and guide are clearing a trail.

tana, is a good example of someone who will pair you up with an outfitter who will cater to your requirements. Atcheson carefully screens outfitters and often hunts with them to get a firsthand look at their operation. If an outfitter doesn't meet Atcheson's standards, Jack drops him. Other reputable agents do likewise.

Should you sign a contract with an outfitter when you book a hunt? For a long time I thought this was a good idea, until some outfitter pals of mine, who run first-class operations, told me that a contract is only a piece of paper and not worth the bother. I guess there's some truth to that, but it might be a good idea to get something in writing before you book.

Here are some questions to ask:

How many hunting days will you get? A 10-day hunt might really mean a day's ride in to camp on a horse, a day's ride out, and only eight days of hunting.

Exactly how will you hunt? If you expect to call elk with a bugle, make sure this is understood. If you expect to ride horseback with a minimum of walking, find out precisely how much walking is involved if you're not in good physical condition. In most elk country the term is climbing rather than walking.

What kinds of extra services are provided? Will the outfitter cape your animal, take your meat to a processor, ship your antlers and cape to a taxidermist? When you arrive in the prescribed town to meet before the hunt, do you stay in a motel and pick up the tab prior to heading out to the hunt area? Or does he put you up for the night or pay the motel bill? In most situations you'll arrive the day before the scheduled hunt and have an extra night on your own.

What kind of gear should you bring? Most outfitters tell you to bring only a rifle, hunting gear such as ammo, binoculars, spotting scope, personal gear, and a sleeping bag. They provide the rest. I always bring along a day pack jammed with odds and ends such as a small flashlight, first-

You can expect good and bad weather on your elk hunt. This guide prepares a horse for his hunter on a snowy day in Idaho.

Packing your gear into camp is a science. Outfitters are expert at transporting equipment on horses and mules.

A big advantage of the outfitted hunt is the option of riding horseback. Animals get you where elk are and save a great deal of time and effort.

aid kit, compass, waterproof matches, rope, hard candy, plastic flagging (to mark a downed elk in dense timber— sometimes even a guide has a tough time finding your animal if you have to return and pack it out), and trail food that I make up myself. (A detailed list of items to take on your elk hunt is included in another chapter.)

Exactly what size elk are you expected to see in his area? This might seem like a silly question, but you should know what the options are before you book. There are plenty of places in elk country where a guide will urge you to shoot the first branch-antlered bull that shows. If that suits you, fine, but if you want to be able to have a chance of selecting a big bull, make sure you're going to be hunting in the right place. Tell the outfitter what you want in the way of a bull. If a trophy is important to you, ask him point blank.

Be aware that when you hunt with an outfitter, the hunt might be more physically demanding than if you hunt on your own. That seems to be contrary to what you might think, but look at it this way. When you're on your own, you hunt at your own pace. You wake up when you want to, hunt as hard as you want to, and select the terrain you hunt. With an outfitter, you hunt according to his schedule. You follow a guide and move along at his pace, perhaps in very steep country.

Don't think an outfitter will provide you with an easy hunt. Some turn out that way, but most don't. All he's doing is packing you into elk country, which can be anywhere from a couple miles to two dozen miles from a road. I've been on high-country elk hunts that were 28 miles from the nearest access point, all of them tough miles on horseback and afoot.

Outfitters often tell me that their hunters are in poor physical condition, so poor that they are unable to hunt effectively. That's a frustrating situation. If a hunter is so out of shape that he can't walk up a slope to peek into a basin on the other side, or walk through timber to get to where elk are living, or at least move quietly without coughing and breaking branches, he won't stand much chance of seeing an elk. And if a hunter can't shoot accurately once an elk is spotted, it's doubly frustrating. Yes, you're paying for the hunt, but the outfitter can't do it all for you. You owe it to him to at least meet the demands of the hunt.

It's important to remember that you're not buying an elk—you're buying a hunt. Whether you get an elk or not is largely up to you.

So far I've been referring to outfitters who pack you in to national forests, where most elk hunting occurs in the West. The reason they pack you in is to get you away from other hunters, which is precisely why the elk are in the remote regions. It's not because the upper elevations hold some special habitat requirement for big elk. Elk don't want to be disturbed, and they'll stay where there's the least human activity. The fact that the high country suits them nicely means that they'll thrive in those lofty domains.

There are also outfitters who offer hunts on large leased

Some outfitters offer drop camps such as this one. You and your gear will be packed in and left. The outfitter returns at a specified time to pack you and your game out.

Elizabeth and Ken Smith, an Idaho outfitter, do a few camp chores. Firewood is always in demand and must be cut constantly.

ranches. In this case, you might ride horseback to secluded areas, but you're more apt to use a vehicle and hunt from private roads, or do a limited amount of climbing. Because the land is leased, the outfitter controls hunter pressure, and elk aren't as hard to find.

Another possibility is to book a drop camp. The outfitter takes you and your companions to a camp he already has set up in the backcountry. You'll ride horses to most drop camps, but some can be reached via a vehicle. The camp will generally have a cook tent, sleeping tent, supply of firewood, stoves in each tent, and cooking utensils. You may or may not have to provide your own food. The outfitter drops you off and arranges to come back and pick you up on a prescribed day. Depending on the terms, he'll pack your game from the kill site down to your vehicle or base camp, or you might have to pack game to the drop camp and he'll take it out from there.

The advantages of drop camps are obvious. You're packed into game country and you can hunt at your leisure. A guide isn't necessary because you're in the vicinity of elk where you camp. The price of a drop camp is much lower than a fully guided hunt.

The disadvantages are the necessity of handling your game and doing your own cooking and camp chores. There's another disadvantage, an important one. Not many outfitters have drop camps because the margin of profit is slim for the outlay of time, equipment, and horseflesh. Also, drop camps are generally not as far back in the boonies as fully guided hunts, and hunters who use a drop camp may come back to the same area another season and hunt on their own, thus offering competition to the outfitter.

How much are you expected to pay an outfitter? A fully guided pack-in hunt can cost $3,000 or more per hunter for 10 days. The cost of a hunt on a leased ranch is variable, depending on the caliber of elk and the management program the rancher or outfitter is using. Drop camps are generally the cheapest and may run from $50 to $100 or more a day per person.

Financial arrangements are usually such that you pay a deposit when you book, with the balance payable when you arrive for the hunt. An outfitter or booking agent often requires a 30 to 50 percent deposit.

One final bit of advice. You will probably spend time on a horse when an outfitter takes you hunting. Read the chapter in this book on horses and hunting. You won't have to be an equestrian expert, but there are basics you should know.

Some of my fondest elk hunting memories surround outfitted hunts. I've made some wonderful friends and have shared experiences that will never be forgotten. That's another plus that should be considered when you plan a hunt. Camaraderie is an important part of hunting. Stories shared in a cook tent or around a smoky campfire never seem to die. To me, that fellowship is as important as killing an elk. I basically like outfitters and their way of life, and I'm betting you will, too.

CHAPTER 16

Do-It-Yourself Elk Hunts

Many sportsmen who haven't been west think an elk hunt is an outfitted affair complete with guides and horses. That's a fine way to go and is recommended for every serious hunter, but it's possible to make an elk foray on your own with a good pal or two.

Before planning an elk hunt on your own, do yourself a big favor and think seriously about the consequences of the hunt if it's successful. You are going to have to transport a lot of weight out of the woods, and the task will be quite an operation if you can't get close to the elk with a horse or vehicle. If that aspect of the hunt doesn't concern you and you're still willing to do it on your own, let's proceed and outline the steps you need to take before heading for elk country.

First, determine the objective of your hunt. Do you want to bring home a trophy or just any bull? What time of the fall do you want to hunt? Have you hunted in the West before or do you know someone who can tell you where to hunt?

Once you've decided on your priorities and selected a

This is Zumbo's elk camp. His horse, Silver; 4X4 pickup truck, and camp trailer. A perfect set-up for elk hunting.

state, immediately inquire about license information so you'll have your applications in before the deadlines. In Wyoming the application for nonresidents has a traditional February 1 deadline. Hunters who wish to try for Montana elk will need to quickly purchase one of the first-come tags reserved for nonresidents. They sell out soon after they go on sale in early April. Other states have similar license requirements, and some have unlimited tags. Learn the details as soon as you can.

Where will you hunt? There are enormous chunks of public land in every western state. Hundreds of millions of acres that do not have posted signs offer excellent hunting opportunities in every environment, from low elevations to alpine forests. Those acres are federal lands administered by the U.S. Forest Service and Bureau of Land Management (BLM).

Obviously, if you've never been in the West and have no contacts, you're better off hunting public land. However,

Bob and Kathy Etling from Missouri make a do-it-yourself hunt in the West every year. They're well-prepared, and are usually successful in their hunting efforts.

some of the best big game hunting is available on private land. It's possible to gain access on private properties, but you might have to pay a trespass fee or buy into a lease. You'll need to find out where good private hunting lands are and who owns them. Local chambers of commerce offices often have lists of landowners who lease hunting rights or sell trespass permits. The best bet is to inquire personally. Ask service station attendants, store clerks, bartenders, and other locals where good hunting areas are. You won't want to be inquiring the day before opening day, of course. Do it well in advance if you can.

Federal wildlife refuges are often overlooked by big game hunters, and some offer hunting for elk. Hunters are usually restricted to certain areas within the refuge, and camping is often permitted in designated areas.

Every western state has Wildlife Management Areas open to hunting. Check with state wildlife agencies for maps and information. Many areas have a quota system on a first-come, first-served basis.

The BLM is the biggest public land agency in North America, with about 350 million acres of land. About half that total is in Alaska; the rest is in the Lower 48. BLM holdings are often considered the "land that nobody wanted." During the great homestead period, settlers took choice valley bottoms and ignored the ridges and mountain slopes. Today those ridges and slopes are superb game country. BLM acreage is important habitat for elk in many regions.

To hunt BLM land, first obtain a map of the area you're interested in. The BLM is divided into districts, which are supervised by a central office in each state. Write to the state office and request a map index that describes the available maps and required fees. Circle the maps you want on the index and send the fees to the state office.

The U.S. Forest Service manages 188 million acres in the United States, 160 million acres of which are in the western states. In the West, 95 national forests offer elk hunting. Unlike BLM lands, national forests are more intensively managed for recreation. Campgrounds are numerous, and access roads into good game country are often plentiful.

For maps and information, write to the appropriate regional office and indicate the forests you want to know more about. The regional office will send a free mini-map, if available, or will inform you of detailed maps that can be acquired for a small fee. A general visitor map shows general features such as forest boundaries, campgrounds, access roads, and other landmarks. Scale is one-half inch or less to the mile. A base map shows more detail, with a scale of one-half inch or more to the mile.

Weather is an important consideration when preparing for a western hunt. Autumn is a fickle period in the West. Balmy, blue skies can quickly change to overcast, nasty skies with temperatures plummeting. Be prepared for every-

The toughest part of a do-it-yourself hunt. Getting elk meat out can be an ordeal. This hunter is carrying a 96-pound hindquarter on his back.

thing and expect the worst. Snow is common after the first of October and is no surprise during September in higher elevations. A blizzard can lay down a foot of snow or more overnight, turning a long-awaited hunt into a fiasco.

When using a vehicle for hunting, be aware of its capabilities. In the West, rugged roads are often the norm in backcountry areas. Small cars might be wonderfully efficient on a cross-country trip, but woefully inadequate on a hunt. Secondary roads might be impassable to vehicles with insufficient power or low clearances.

If you must use a vehicle unsuitable for back-road travel, there are plenty of places where you can park along all-weather paved roads or major gravel roads and hunt from them. You'll need to walk farther and climb higher than in more remote areas to get away from hunters, however.

Most westerners drive a four-wheel-drive rig. Despite the advantages of backcountry vehicles, however, they get stuck just as badly as a passenger car and often worse. The old saying that a 4WD will get you mired farther back in the boonies is accurate. Hunters often push vehicles beyond their limits just to gain a few more yards up the road.

The most valuable use of a 4WD is its ability to get you into prime hunting country, where there is less competition from other hunters. Hunters who can't penetrate good areas will need to spend much of their time walking to them. For example, a forest road might leave a paved highway at 5500 feet elevation, but you might need to drive 25 or 30 miles on it to get to elk at about 8500 feet or so. A muddy or rocky spot in the road might stymie your ability to get to game country, and you might be left a dozen miles or more short of the prime hunting area.

If you don't want to spend the extra money required for gasoline for a 4WD, you can travel west in an economy rig and rent a 4WD when you get to the area of your choice. In popular hunting spots, make reservations for a 4WD well in advance of hunting season. Call the local chamber of commerce and ask who rents vehicles close to the hunting area.

Jim Zumbo carries his camp on his back in 1975. He still back-packs for elk, but more slowly and carefully.

Many hunters tow 4WD vehicles behind a motorhome or pickup camper.

When heading for the backcountry, be sure to bring extra gasoline—more than you think you'll need. Many hunters have a second tank installed in their vehicle. A good rule of thumb is to have at least 50 gallons of gas before heading out for an extended trip.

Another chapter tells how to get meat out, but let me say here that there are a number of places to rent horses, especially around popular elk hunting areas. Many hunters pursue elk afoot and rent a horse to transport the meat. The chapter on outfitters gives details on horses and their use.

The most economical way to get to the West is to drive out with two companions. Three hunters can fit in a vehicle nicely and can take turns driving. From the East Coast, you can make a trip to Colorado or Wyoming in 40 to 50 hours. Many hunters haul camp trailers or pickup campers. A roomy tent is adequate and allows more mobility. You should prepare to leave a hunting area if no game is sighted or sign is scarce. A tent can be quickly taken down and set up in a new area.

Most hunters fail to scout properly, especially if they make a long drive and have limited time to hunt. Ideally, you should try to make camp at least two days before the opener to determine the availability of game. Get out early in the morning to locate elk. Do not, however, overdo your scouting efforts. If you're too persistent, you can chase game out of the country before the opener. Simply satisfy yourself that animals are in the area you've elected to hunt, and try to determine feeding areas without spooking elk.

Putting together a do-it-yourself western trip is going to take a coordinated effort, but you can do it if you want to. Life is a matter of priorities. If you're tired of staring at elk heads on the wall of a tavern or sportsman's club and yearn to collect one of your own, now's the time to start planning. And when it finally comes together and you get your first glimpse of the magnificent West, you'll be glad you made the big decision to do it.

CHAPTER 17

What to Bring on an Elk Hunt

Because elk hunting often involves a long hunt in a remote area, or at least a hunt in the mountains where weather can cause problems, you must be properly equipped before you leave home.

Here's a checklist of gear you should bring, and I'll assume space and weight will limit your cargo. That's almost always the case, especially if you're with an outfitter and you're heading into the backcountry with horses. I'll also list essentials as well as a few luxury items that take little space and will make your hunt much more enjoyable.

SLEEPING GEAR

A sleeping bag is a personal item that you're expected to provide, unless you're staying in a lodge with beds and linens. In that case, you will be so advised. But 99 percent of the elk hunters in the world will doze in a sleeping bag.

Do not bring a down bag if you're tent camping. Though I dearly love down and my favorite bag is a wonderful down affair, I've cussed it a dozen times when it got wet. Down is hard to dry and it's cold and clammy when it's wet. It's far better to sleep in a bag filled with manmade fibers (much as I hate to admit it), such as Quallofil, Hollofil, Fiberfil, or any of the synthetic materials. They are comfortable when damp, and they dry quickly.

Bring a bag rated for very cold temperatures, despite the fact that the outfitter claims you'll be sleeping in a heated tent. Be assured that the fire in the stove will go out a couple hours after you retire, and the air temperature inside the tent will quickly match that of the air outside. I know plenty of hunters who brought summer bags on an elk hunt and spent many miserable nights because of it.

Put your sleeping bag in a heavy-duty plastic trash bag, and then put it in another one just for good measure. The trash bag will keep it dry while it's being transported into camp. Sleeping bags have a way of getting damp if the weather is moist, no matter how carefully they're packed.

If you expect to sleep on a cot, which is normally the case in tent camps, ask the outfitter if he provides foam pads for the cots. If not, bring your own. It will make all the difference in the world for sleeping comfort. Besides providing the extra cushion, the cot will provide insulation beneath you. Though you might have a warm sleeping bag rated at minus-zero temperatures, there's no loft underneath because your weight compresses the bag. As a result, the cold air in the tent will make you most uncomfortable.

Bring a small pillow. Yes, this is not necessary, but it's a nice luxury that takes little space and you'll appreciate it after a tough day of hunting.

CLOTHING

Prepare for every possible kind of weather, because you'll probably get it. I'll start from the skin out, and suggest proper apparel for different weather conditions.

If you're hunting early in the season and the weather is

Vin Sparano, OUTDOOR LIFE's Executive Editor, is dressed appropriately on this Idaho elk hunt. The day was balmy but promised rain. He's wearing two wool shirts, woolen trousers, and waterproof boots.

balmy, wear whatever trousers are comfortable and several lightweight shirts. I usually wear a couple flannel shirts over an undershirt. If the weather turns extremely warm, I shuck a shirt and stuff it in my daypack—which I *always* carry. For footwear, I wear a pair of cotton or light woolen socks, and a pair of lightweight, waterproof hiking boots. I carry a heavy woolen jacket in my daypack along with gloves in the event that a cold front moves in.

If the weather turns cold, I wear polypropylene longjohns, warm trousers, two wool shirts, a down vest, and a woolen jacket. I usually wear two pair of woolen socks and insulated, waterproof boots. On my hands I wear a pair of lightweight cotton gloves topped by a pair of leather gloves. A warm hat protects my head, and a bandanna around my throat keeps my neck warm.

These Wyoming guides huddle around a cheery fire during a break in the hunt. Be sure you have warm clothing. You won't hunt well if you're cold and miserable.

For late-season hunting in snow and rain, I wear lots of wool. First, the polypropylene longjohns, then wool pants, wool shirts, and wool jacket. Two pair of wool socks encased in a pair of pacs with felt liners, leather uppers and rubber bottoms keep my feet warm as toast. A Gore-Tex slicker or overcoat is a must to keep me dry, and gloves and hat keep the rest of me warm. I like plenty of wool in wet weather because wool wicks when it's damp and actually retains heat and keeps you warm. Wool is more expensive than most other garments, but it's worth its weight in gold when you're out hunting and the weather is wet and miserable.

As far as a total list of clothes to bring, be sure you have plenty of socks and underwear, longjohns, four or five warm shirts, two or three pair of trousers, gloves, hat, a warm overcoat or heavy jacket, rain jacket and rain pants, and a pair of mocassins or casual shoes to lounge around in camp besides hunting boots. If your clothes get wet while you're hunting, you can usually dry them quickly near a wood-stove.

Dirt is another matter. Don't strive for extreme cleanliness in elk camp by bringing a dozen shirts and trousers. You can keep your body clean with plenty of soap and warm water, but don't fuss about your looks. No one will care how you look, because you'll all look rather unkept and untidy by the time the hunt nears its end anyway.

If you're worried about blisters or sores on your feet, bring a supply of moleskin. It might very well save the hunt if your feet give you problems.

A note about hunter orange apparel. Most western states require orange for safety reasons. Don't buy a cheap 99-cent plastic vest. It will shred and tear the first time you walk or ride through vegetation. Buy a good article of clothing and avoid nylon because it's noisy in the brush. The same goes for raingear. Buy sturdy apparel that will last, not an inexpensive garment that will rip and tear easily.

PERSONAL GEAR

As far as a guideline for personal gear, bring whatever items you normally use in your bathroom at home. Store your articles in a sturdy toilet kit that is big enough to accommodate your needs. You might also want to bring along extra items, such as a laxative, diarrhea preventative, antacid medication, effervescent tablets, aspirin, cough syrup, and any medication you might need. If you take prescribed medication regularly, be certain you have an adequate supply.

If you enjoy a libation before or after dinner, bring your own. Outfitters normally don't provide liquor. One bottle of your favorite should suffice. Don't overdo it and don't expect

An ideal elk camp. These nonresident hunters use an economy truck and a tent to keep their costs low.

the outfitter to pack in a case of wine or beer for you.

By all means, have a dependable flashlight. Of late, I've been hauling around two or three of the disposable type. They're small, lightweight, and easy to use and store.

A first-aid kit is handy for minor cuts and bruises. The outfitter will have one, but I like to carry my own as well.

CAMP GEAR

If you're hunting on your own, you'll need plenty of equipment. A warm shelter is the primary consideration. Camp vehicles such as trailers, cab-over campers, and motorhomes solve the comfort problem, but if you must use a tent, you'll have to bring extra equipment.

Make sure the tent is waterproof, even if the manufacturer claims it to be so. If it's supposed to be, don't believe it. If you read the instructions that come with the tent, you'll

Bring plenty of tools to care for your meat, hide, and cape. Take good care of your elk, because it will quickly spoil. Zumbo fleshes a hide before salting it down.

see where each seam must be sealed, including Gore-Tex tents that are superior to anything else on the market. Many tents will come with a tube of sealant in the packaging. If not, buy a tube. Before the elk hunt, set the tent up in your backyard and seal it thoroughly. Every stitch must be treated.

Cots are a good idea because they keep you up off the ground to avoid moisture and are comfortable. They take up space, but they're worth it.

A heater is not a luxury but is often essential. A collapsible woodstove will suffice, and it doubles as a cooking stove. A catalytic heater works well, but I've yet to see one keep a tent warm during very cold weather, especially if the wind is blowing. A regular camp stove that runs on white

These elk hunters use small aircraft to get to their jump-off point.
Outfitters will probably suggest you keep your gear to a minimum. Pack accordingly—they're serious!

gas or propane is adequate for cooking. Have a plentiful
supply of fuel on hand.

A light source inside the tent is necessary, and I've yet
to see an elk camp without a good old one- or two-mantle
lantern. I have a half-dozen in my garage, and I've become
enamored with the propane model that uses a disposable
fuel tank rather than the white gas model, which is usually
temperamental and messy to fill with white gas. I'll admit,
though, that the latter is traditional and gives you a few
seconds to jump into the sleeping bag when you turn it off at
night. The propane type goes out immediately when you
turn the knob.

Firewood is often an important consideration around elk
camp. Bring a sharp ax as well as a file to keep it sharp.
You'll no doubt bring along a favorite camp knife, as well as
one to carry in your pocket.

As far as equipment to cut up your elk with, check the list in the chapter on how to get an elk out of the woods. Be sure you've got everything you need, because that project will no doubt be the toughest work you'll do on the hunt, besides hauling the meat to a road or to camp. You'll also need to figure out a way to get your meat home. That's also described elsewhere in this book.

THE DAYPACK

I bring along a daypack wherever I hunt. It holds a small first-aid kit; a survival kit that includes waterproof matches, mirror, candle, fishhooks, fishing line, and other items; a bag of hard candy; trail food that I make up myself (assorted goodies such as sunflower seeds, raisins, coconut, almonds, peanuts, etc.); reliable flashlight; space blanket; wool jacket; film; 50 feet of rope; small block and tackle; collapsible meat saw; sharpening stone; and extra cartridges. In addition to all this I place my camera where it's handy.

Many outfitters will tell you to keep the total weight of your gear under a certain limit. Follow their advice. Many will also provide a checklist of equipment to bring along on your hunt. Heed those instructions as well. When packing gear, use soft duffel bags, never hard suitcases, and bring a soft case for your gun. Chances are you'll put your gun in the scabbard when you leave the trailhead if you're riding a horse, and I guarantee no outfitter will pack a hard gun case into camp.

If you're unsure of what gear to bring, consult a friend who is an experienced elk hunter, or ask your outfitter or booking agent. They should be able to answer your questions. When in doubt, the key is to keep warm and dry. If you can manage to do both on your elk hunt, everything else will fall into place. An uncomfortable hunter is a poor hunter. Make it easy on yourself and be prepared, but don't overdo it with unnecessary gear.

CHAPTER 18

Avoid Getting Lost

Elk woods are usually vast expanses of landscape that have no comparison to other parts of the country. You might walk for dozens of miles and never strike a road, and most of the terrain will be up and down. A sea of evergreen timber will quickly swallow you, and you could easily travel too far during a day's hunt and not have enough daylight to walk back out.

Consistently successful elk hunters walk miles of tough topography. They don't fear the woods, which is a very basic reason why they readily find elk. If you're continually afraid of being lost and are reluctant to attack elk country, your chances of scoring will be slim to none. You must cover plenty of acres to find animals, and you can't do it if you're hesitant about leaving a road, trail, or creek.

While it's always important to try to become familiar with the area you're planning to hunt before the season, that's not always possible. In fact, very few hunters actually scout prior to the season. Many have no idea where they are when they step into the woods opening morning.

Such was the case with me two decades ago. I was hunting Colorado with relatives and friends, and we arrived late the night before opening day. At 5 a.m., after a harrowing Jeep ride up a horrible road etched into a steep mountainside, I was instructed to hunt toward a certain ridge and meet the rest of the party for lunch. I had no map and had no idea where the ridge was. Someone pointed to it in the black of night, and I did my best to find it when daylight finally broke. I didn't hunt well because I spent too much time and brainpower trying to figure out where I was.

I made a vow at that point that I'd never put myself in that situation again, and I haven't. Though I've gone to strange areas the night before a hunt, I hunt according to my rules instead of someone else's, unless I'm with a guide and we figure a strategy.

That brings up another point. If you're on a guided hunt and your guide suggests you hunt alone and meet him at a particular spot, be sure you're up to it before agreeing. If your sense of direction is poor and you're unsure where the

These hunters check a map before setting out in the woods. Order the best, updated maps you can before your hunt.

guide wants to meet you, don't be afraid to refuse or at least come up with another option. Most guides won't leave you, but some might ask you to hunt alone from Point A to Point B because it will be more effective to do so.

If a guide asks you to make a solo walk, he'll generally suggest that you follow a creek, a well-defined ridge, or another conspicuous landmark. If you want no part of hunting by yourself, make it immediately clear to your guide before you leave camp the first day.

In the event that you're hunting on your own, bring along a *good* map as well as a compass, and know how to use both. Note the emphasis on the word good. Some maps aren't worth the paper they're printed on. Buy the very best available. I like topographic maps because they show detail, contours, various land features, and are easy to read. You can buy them in bookstores, sporting goods stores, or you can send away for them.

Virtually every square yard in North America is plotted on a topo map. If you want maps east of the Mississippi River (not specifically for elk, but for general hunting purposes), write to the U.S. Geological Survey, 536 National Center, Reston, VA 22092. For maps west of the Mississippi, write to the U.S. Geological Survey, Box 25046, Federal Center, Denver, CO 80225. Map costs vary, depending on the size and scale, but are generally less than $5 each. Request an index when you write initially so you can determine the specific topo maps you'll need.

It's likely that you'll be hunting elk in a national forest. If so, Forest Service offices have maps of their forests available, some free and some for a small fee. Check the state-by-state directory in this book and write to the national forest you intend to hunt.

Having a good map doesn't mean much unless you know how to read it. It's surprising how easy it is to get turned around when using a map. Unlike highway maps where most roads are numbered, a forest map shows various roads, many of which are not identified by signs on the ground. In

Gloomy, cloudy days like these require compass assistance to find your way around the elk woods. Be sure you can use a compass correctly before you hunt.

fact, many roads are not on the map at all, adding still more confusion.

A map in itself is not all you'll need to find your way around the elk woods. Without a compass, you won't have much hope finding elk unless you have a superb sense of direction and are willing to penetrate thick stands of timber where landmarks are absent.

A few years back I was hunting in Montana and my party was accidentally left without horses due to a misunderstanding with another member of the party who was supposed to leave our horses in a predetermined spot. The horses weren't where they were supposed to be, and we walked out in the moonlight. We were sure we were headed in the right direction when it finally occurred to us that we were going exactly the opposite way we should have been. One of my pals walked into an opening and checked the Big

Before hunting, scout if you can and look for landmarks, as these hunters are doing. If you can get an idea of the lay of the land before you hunt, you have an advantage.

Dipper to find the North Star. At the same time I pulled out my compass and immediately realized we were wrong. Our mistake cost us a couple hours and some pride; we should have checked our direction occasionally as we trekked through the snow.

A compass is a simple tool, yet many hunters are baffled when it comes to using one. Most of the confusion arises when you need to refer to the compass to get out of an area you've been hunting.

Reading a compass is incredibly easy. All you need to do is hold it flat so the needle can move freely, and turn your body around until the needle hovers over the N, which stands for north. With that done, the space in front of you is north. Other directions are relative to north; i.e., south is behind you, east is to your right, west is to your left.

The simplest way to avoid getting lost is to follow a direction or bearing into the woods, and when you're done hunting, you simply reverse the bearing 180 degrees and come back out. Unfortunately, you can't do that and hunt elk effectively because you should be doing a great deal of meandering that will complicate your course. When you walk ridges, cross into different drainages, and otherwise wander around looking for elk sign, you won't be able to simply reverse your route because you've wound about so much that you're far from the starting area.

That's where a map comes in. When you hunt, refer to the map frequently, and classify your journey in a series of separate events. For example, say you leave the truck and walk west into some timber until you climb out onto a ridge. Then you hunt north along the ridge for about a half-mile, drop down and follow a creek for a full mile, and stillhunt for the rest of the day. Say you've located fresh elk sign and you want to spend time in the area. By staying in the drainage where the creek flows down, you know that all you have to do to return to the truck is follow the creek back up to the ridge. That's event number one. When you reach the ridge, you turn south and walk along it for a half-mile. That's event number two. Then you walk east through the timber until you hit the road that your vehicle is parked on. That's event number three.

But let's say an elk fouls up your plans. You hear a bull bugle in another drainage, or you come across fresh tracks that lead you out of the creek valley you're using as a basic reference. When that happens, you hunt according to whatever strategy lends itself to catching up to the elk, but you constantly note the landforms around you. If you cross into another drainage, note where your friendly creek from event one is and be sure you can get back to it. To help keep track of your route, refer to your map constantly, and make notes with a pen or pencil.

Another way to hunt and not get lost is to forget about keeping track of events and strike into the forest in a general direction with a long baseline to use as a reference point. The baseline can be a river, straight stretch of a creek, a straight road, or even a highway. By doing so, you can hunt all day, cross into a half-dozen drainages, and walk out by just reversing your direction wherever you happen to be when you decide to head for the vehicle.

For example, say you park your truck on a forest road and the map shows the road runs north and south for several miles in front and behind you. You turn east into the forest and hunt to your heart's content. When it's time to head out you use your compass and head west until you strike the road.

Another possibility is to use gravity as your guide. Say you locate a likely looking timbered area and you can see a ridge far up on top. A road or stream runs around the base of the mountain and the ridge becomes your objective. You simply hunt uphill with the ridge as your known landmark, whether you can see it or not as you're hunting. When you decide to head back to the vehicle, you simply walk down until you come to the road or stream at the base of the mountain.

Some hunters are unnerved anytime they're out of sight or hearing of civilization, or if they aren't physically on a road or trail. If you're bothered by the emptiness and the uncertainty of the woods, try hunting near a major highway or within earshot of a noisy sawmill, oil rig, or other activity. The fact that you can constantly hear human noises and know exactly how to get out might relax you so you'll hunt better. Don't rule out seeing elk where you can hear people sounds, because elk will be perfectly comfortable as long as they're undisturbed. That's another plus to hunting near habitation. Hunters often ignore those spots, thinking they need to be in more remote areas.

It's possible to walk along a well-marked forest trail to penetrate the backcountry, then leave the trail and hunt where human access is minimal. Be assured that elk know where those busy trails are and will avoid them in the daytime. You'll need to get off the beaten path to find animals. Most trails run up canyon bottoms or along ridgetops and are easy to find again once you've left them and come back.

If you want to get away from people, trails, and noises, you can use the toilet tissue technique. Carry a quantity of tissue in your daypack or pocket and place a square on a branch where it can be seen from a distance. Use white tissues because they will rapidly decompose if you miss a few as you collect them on your way back out. By marking a tissue trail you can go anywhere and retrace your steps. Be attentive if it's windy, raining or snowing. Wind could blow your markers to the ground, and rain or snow could make them tough to see.

Some hunters use plastic flagging to mark a trail. That's not a good idea, because uncollected strips will flutter for years and clutter the woods.

Despite all your precautions, compass, map, and sense of direction, you might find yourself hopelessly turned around with night fast approaching. Then what?

It's easy for me to suggest that you keep calm, collect your wits, and be cool, because I'm sitting here in my office writing this and advice is simple to give. It's also easy for you to read this advice from a comfortable chair, nod your head, and agree wholeheartedly. But it's quite another thing to be out there in the woods by yourself and fight the fear and panic that wells in your being when you realize you're in a strange, primitive place with no immediate hope of getting out. Your brain will immediately conjure the worst— you'll never get out and will become a statistic.

The first thing to do is to think positively. Someone will be looking for you as soon as your companions realize you're missing. In that regard, always tell someone where you intend to hunt so they have an idea where to start looking. If you do a solo hunt over the course of several days, talk to a forest officer, tell him or her where your vehicle is going to be parked and the day you expect to be out. If your rig is there past the due date, they can start a search.

While I'm on the subject, I might suggest that it's foolish to hunt by yourself in a rugged area. Too many things can go wrong. And if everything goes right and you kill an elk, you'll have a tough time getting it out by yourself.

I have to admit that I don't follow my own advice in this matter. Every year I hunt elk by myself. I leave the horse in the pasture and carry my gear on my back. It's a personal challenge, and I suppose I do it to prove to myself that I can. I tell my wife where I intend to hunt, as well as how many days I expect to be gone. Now and then, however, I'll take off for a strange area in a neighboring state and have no idea where I'll hunt. I'll wander around, talk to people, and find a likely area. When I settle on a place to hunt, I'll give it a try for a day or two, then move on to another place if necessary. As soon as I figure where I'll hunt, I call home and tell my wife I'll be somewhere in a certain national forest, and if I'm not home on a prescribed date to call the ranger and have them look for my truck. So far that hasn't been necessary, but if I ever broke a leg or got hurt or impossibly lost, I'd want to know that someone will come looking sooner or later.

But let's get back to you and your predicament of being stuck in the woods with night coming on. If you know about where you are and can follow a creek or ridge in the dark with the assistance of a flashlight, you might be able to carefully find your way out. But if you're turned around, your number one priority is to admit that you're going to spend the night in the woods. Don't fight that rationale, because you'll just make it harder on yourself.

Once you've convinced yourself that you're there until morning and someone will come looking, make preparations to spend the night. Use the remaining daylight to gather a big supply of wood, and get a nice cheery fire going. With that done, find a comfortable place to lie down. You probably won't sleep much, but you might catch a few winks here and there between tossing wood on the fire during the night. Keep the fire going. Besides the warmth it provides, it will help your brain deal with the situation a bit better. A fire lifts the spirit and suggests security.

I'm assuming that you have matches. *Never* go elk hunting without matches, no matter how short a hunt you expect. And make sure your matches are in a waterproof container. Better yet, buy waterproof matches, which are now sold in almost every sporting goods store. You can hold them underwater as long as you like, then take them out and strike them; they work. Use them.

When morning comes, stay by your campfire a couple hours to give searchers a chance to find you. If no help comes, think long and hard about where you are and try to recreate the drainages and ridges you've crossed. Slowly work your way through the woods if you think you can find a landmark. You might climb to a ridgetop and spot something familiar from the top. If you hear a chainsaw in the distance, immediately pinpoint the location as best you can and take a compass bearing. If you don't have a compass, concentrate on the direction the sound is coming from and head for it as quickly as you safely can. A chainsaw probably means a road, and if you can move rapidly enough you'll find people.

The standard signal of distress is three gunshots fired rapidly. If you hear three shots, respond by firing your gun three times. Don't move, because searchers will home in on your location and will head for you. Remember that they'll be walking, looking for you, so don't try to find them.

The best way to survive besides keeping your wits is to have essential gear in a daypack. In another chapter I've detailed the equipment you should have for any eventuality.

Don't be unprepared. Elk woods are big, and they can be unforgiving. Don't ever forget it.

CHAPTER 19

Get in Shape for Elk

I've heard the lament dozens of times from outfitters: "If only that hunter was in shape he could have killed an elk."

Elk hunting is the toughest, meanest, nastiest form of hunting in North America. That's not only my opinion but that of respected, veteran elk hunters who have many more miles under their boot soles than I do.

You might have to do some tricky cliff-scaling to stalk a mountain goat, and you'll huff to find a Bighorn ram, but day in and day out you won't hunt as hard for anything else as you will for an elk.

Unfortunately, too many hunters have no idea what they're getting in to. Perhaps outdoor writers like myself have been guilty of portraying elk hunting in a simplistic scenario, such as the bugle hunt in which the bull is called into range and shot by the waiting hunter. To be sure, this is a romantic version of the pursuit, but a minor one. If the truth were known, less than 10 percent of the elk hunters afield try for an elk during the bugle season. Most seasons are held after the rut, and the only method that works is to dig elk out of the timber where they're hiding, or look for

This hunter looks for elk at 10,000 feet, not an uncommon elevation to hunt elk in the Rockies. At this altitude, you need to be in good condition to walk and climb. It may take a few days to acclimate yourself if you live at low elevations.

them in an undisturbed place where they aren't bothered by
humans.

I usually figure on walking six to 10 miles a day when
I'm elk hunting, and a good share of that distance is uphill.
I'm not actually hunting all that time but merely looking for
fresh sign, and that might be tough to do in typical elk
country where you're trying to find an elusive herd in a
huge chunk of land.

That's a basic part of elk hunting: looking rather than
hunting. Once you find what you're looking for, you slow
down and hunt.

There are exceptions to the hard-hunting rule, and I
know a couple that are amusing. A hunter I'm acquainted
with drank too much the eve of opening morning and slept
instead of going out hunting with his pals. He arose about
10 a.m., drove his pickup down the road, parked it in the
sun, and dozed behind the wheel. At one point he woke up to
see a six-point bull elk running full-tilt down the mountain
right at the truck. The bleary-eyed man grabbed his rifle,
jumped out, and killed the elk at a range of 125 yards.

Another time, a hunter sat in camp making stew when
he heard a commotion in the nearby forest. Picking up his
rifle, he investigated and saw a herd of elk running through
the timber. The man spotted a four-point bull and killed it
with one shot less than 30 yards from camp.

But these are rare occurrences. They make for humor-
ous campfire palaver, and certainly aren't indicative of elk
hunting. It's a tough, tough activity, pure and simple.

With that in mind, it becomes an absolute fact that in
order to be an effective elk hunter, you must be in good
physical condition. And don't think you'll get off easy if you
hire an outfitter. You'll end up working harder, because
you'll be following a guide who will set a pace according to
your physical condition. Most guides, however, will push just
a bit to make you move a little faster and hunt a little
harder. If you were hunting on your own, you could move
according to your wishes, and even so you won't get near elk

If you hunt with this guide, you'll need to be in good shape to keep up with him. Make sure your guide maintains a comfortable pace you can live with.

Elk hunting is tough, tough work. Be sure you're in physical condition before tackling the western mountains.

if you can't cover mountainous terrain in a reasonable
amount of time.

You should make preparations for your elk hunt long
before the season. Don't start getting in shape in July for a
September hunt. Begin your exercise program at least six
months to a year before the hunt.

My good friend and hunting buddy, Dr. Parker Davies,

This hunter took this bull on a ridgetop. If he wasn't in good shape as well as an alert hunter, he would never have taken this elk.

M.D., suggests that every person over 35 have a stress EKG before starting a strenuous exercise program or leaving for an elk hunt.

I'm not going to describe an exercise program for you. That's something you can work out with your doctor in accordance to your lifestyle and exercise preferences. Just be aware that you're going to be placing a great demand on three parts of your body: your heart, lungs, and legs. Your lungs and legs will protest immediately when the going gets rough, but your heart might suffer serious damage with tragic consequences if you aren't physically prepared for the rigors of the hunt. Every year, hunters die from heart attacks because of the sudden exertion.

Every year I see hunters woefully out of shape, and I know immediately that they'll never see an elk, much less kill one. Besides being physically unfit, overweight hunters are a liability to others as well as to themselves. There aren't many mountain horses that can pack a 280-pound hunter complete with clothes, gear, saddle, and tack. A heavy hunter will sore horses right and left, and the outfitter will dread the day he booked him. I've known it to happen many times.

Do yourself a big favor. Either get in shape, book an elk hunt where you can hunt from a vehicle (very rare), make an elk hunt on your own where you can hunt at your own leisurely pace, or don't invest time and money hunting elk. This might sound sarcastic, and I don't intend to be, but you'll end up the loser all the way around if you're in sad physical condition and try a strenuous elk hunt. You might not believe me now as you read this, but I promise you'll remember this advice when you're dragging up a steep hill on wobbly legs, gasping for air, with your chest pounding at every step.

This doesn't mean you should never try an elk hunt if you aren't in good condition. Plenty of hunters are in advanced years and simply cannot improve their health. There are still ways to hunt without overdoing it. Apply for limited entry areas where hunters are restricted and elk aren't so tough to find. Hunt elk during the bugle season when they're much more active and you stand a chance of calling one in with a minimum of effort. Try for an elk tag in special low-elevation hunts where you won't have to do a great deal of climbing. Or apply for a late elk tag in a unit that has a hunt during the migration season where you might not have to walk long distances.

Use good judgment in the elk woods, and don't push your body beyond its limitations. You have everything to lose, including your life.

CHAPTER 20

Horseback Hunting

Elk and horseback hunting go together like peanut butter and jelly. Horses do two nice things for you: They get you into the outback where elk are, and they haul your elk out of the boonies. Each year, I love my horse more and more. When I was younger and more foolish, I hauled pieces of elk out on my back, but now I'm a bit wiser. A horse is a great asset in elk woods, pure and simple.

Each year, thousands of urban hunters who show up in hunting camps are totally unfamiliar with horses. Many don't have the slightest idea of how to handle animals and are nervous around them.

A typical hunt scenario goes like this. You and other hunters arrive in town and are driven to the trailhead. The wrangler and guides bundle gear and lash it onto pack animals. Riding horses are saddled, and a young man with a battered cowboy hat and well-worn Levi's hands you a pair of reins attached to a horse.

"This is Diablo," the cowboy says. "You'll ride him to camp."

"How far is camp?" you ask.

Zumbo's horse, Silver, ready for an elk hunt, adorned with orange streamers. You never know what other hunters will think you and your horse are.

"Oh, 'bout 17 miles," he answers. "Purty easy trail, just a couple real bad spots. You'll be eatin' T-bones in five hours or so."

At that moment you wonder about the wisdom of planning this trip. You could be hunting whitetails on rolling woodlands, or partridge on a back forty, or just taking care of some neglected chores around the house. But here you are, on a Wild West hunt, about to become intimate with a horse named Diablo.

Several hours later you ride into hunting camp, amazed that you survived the journey. It wasn't as bad as you thought, and Diablo earned your respect. Except for some aching muscles and some scary sections of trail that momentarily unnerved you, you're none the worse for wear.

A horseback hunt is nothing to fear or be concerned

If you hunt elk with an outfitter, you'll probably use a horse. Don't feel inadequate if you don't have any horse riding experience. Other members of your party will probably be in the same situation. Ask a guide for help when you need it.

about, though you can make it easier on yourself by knowing a few basic rules of horse handling.

For starters, be assured that an outfitter will provide you with a well-broke horse that is easily handled. There should be no exceptions to that rule, because the last thing an outfitter needs or wants is an extra problem on the trail or in a backcountry camp. It's his moral obligation to supply you with a trained horse.

If you haven't been around horses much, don't be afraid to tell the wrangler or guide. He's used to clients who are unfamiliar with horses, and your pride shouldn't keep you from asking questions.

Here are some tips you should know:

First, make sure you have adequate clothing readily available before riding into camp. It might be balmy when

Before heading into elk country, tie a jacket on your saddle as Vin Sparano is doing. You'll save a lot of grief by not having to unpack horses to get a coat if the weather turns cold on the trail.

This guide is preparing a saddle horse for his hunter. Outfitters provide well-broke, well-mannered horses to hunters. To do otherwise would be asking for unwanted trouble.

you leave the vehicles, but chances are excellent that the temperature will drop considerably before you reach camp. Retrieve a warm jacket from your duffel and tie it behind you on the saddle. If you don't, you'll have two options if it cools off while you're riding. You can shiver and shake, or you can ask the outfitter or guide to unpack your gear and get your jacket while you're riding along the trail.

Be aware that the latter option will immediately cause much grief and consternation. Packing is a highly specialized skill; the packs are weighed or carefully estimated so they are equally balanced before being lashed to pack animals. The rope work and knots will impress a sailor, and your guide will be extremely unhappy if he has to halt the entire packstring, dismantle a pair of packs, find your jacket, and redo the whole works.

If you aren't hardened to periods of long riding, wear

longjohns under your trousers. They'll help protect your legs and thighs from chafing.

As soon as you climb into the saddle, be sure your stirrups are set at the right length. Most guides will check this out, but a few won't. If the stirrups seem uncomfortable, tell the guide. He'll adjust them for you.

Getting into a saddle might seem like child's play, but it can be a major undertaking if you're short and the horse is tall, and if you aren't agile. The project will be even more of an ordeal if the ground isn't level and you attempt to hoist yourself up from the downhill side.

There are several ways to beat the problem. Lead your horse alongside a rock, log, sidehill, or high mound of earth. Stand on the high spot and climb into the saddle. Another technique is to turn the horse around and get on from the uphill side. The simplest method of all, but one that most novices think can't be done, is to get on the animal from its right side. It's a popular belief that you must climb into a saddle from only the left side. That might be true in movies, TV shows, equestrian parks or other civilized places, but usually not in the mountains. Most horses are trained to be mounted from either side. If in doubt, ask the guide.

Once you're in the saddle, you're in total command. It's up to you to control the horse. Generally, all you need to do is hold on. The horse will follow the animals in front of it.

If you know nothing about reining, be sure to find out how before you head down the trail. It's a simple matter to learn; just a few seconds of instructions will allow you to handle your horse. You'll need to know how to turn a horse right or left, and how to make it halt, which are easy procedures.

As you ride along, trust your horse. Invariably there will be places along the trail that will seem suicidal. Stream crossings, narrow trails along steep mountainsides, boulders and logs in the trail, and other obstacles might turn your knuckles white as you hold on for dear life. Your horse will no doubt maneuver through these bad spots with ease, and you'll be impressed with the animal's abilities.

No horse is accident-free, however. Place your feet in the stirrups so you can quickly jump out of the saddle in an emergency. Don't snug your boots tightly into the stirrups, but put light pressure on your toes. You'll probably be wearing hunting boots rather than cowboy boots, which is all the more reason to avoid wedging your feet into the stirrups. Cowboy boots are tapered and made for riding, but hunting boots aren't.

If the trail seems mighty unsafe and your horse is slipping constantly, don't be afraid to get off and lead the animal. You can walk a horse just about as fast as other members of your party who are riding. Don't be embarrassed about doing so, either. It doesn't bother me a bit to dismount and walk my horse down steep trails or along those that are icy. I've taken lots of spills off horses, almost always when I shouldn't have been riding.

Never tighten a cinch if the saddle seems to be loose and rides heavily to one side. Let your guide do it. Plenty of horses are badly sored because inexperienced riders draw the cinch too tight.

You'll quickly notice that horses are gregarious beasts. If you try to ride off alone away from the other horses, or halt on the trail by yourself, you'll have an upset animal under you. It will no doubt protest and whinny, and you must be firm. About the only time you'll need to get off alone is to make a nature stop or take a picture of the group. If possible, have another rider lead your horse while you carry on with your task, or ask the guide to stop momentarily.

When you must walk behind a horse, greet it by calling its name and gently slap in on the back to let the animal know you're there. If you startle a horse, it could kick and cause serious injuries.

During the hunt, you'll be tying your horse to trees frequently. Let the guide tie the horse for you if you don't

Dr.Parker N. Davies, M.D., Jim Zumbo's hunting pal, adjusts a saddle pannier on his pack horse in preparation for an elk hunt. Packing is an art, and is learned only through experience.

know how. Generally, you tie the animal head-high with the halter rope. Leave just enough rope so the horse can stand freely and move its head, but not enough so it can entangle its legs.

As you cross streams, your horse might want a drink. In most cases you should allow it to do so unless your guide tells you not to. If the animals are thirsty and several hunters ride up to a creek or lake, the horses will push and shove one another as they water. Lead your horse away from the others a bit so it has room.

You'll invariably be doing some night riding during the hunt. If it's heavily overcast, you won't be able to see the ground beneath you. This is a time that you must really trust your horse. Be assured that most horses have excellent night vision, no matter how black the outdoors gets. It might seem downright scary to sit on an animal as it maneuvers across obstacles and along narrow trails in the darkness, but you shouldn't worry. To protect your eyes, wear a hat with a brim and pull it down over your face. Keep your head down and let your horse carry you along at its own pace. Hold the reins lightly, and don't attempt to turn the horse in the dark. It will follow the horse ahead of it, and you will never be asked to lead the group. Your guide should always be ahead of you. Never turn on your flashlight unless there's an urgent reason. The light will temporarily blind the horse.

Stay out of the way when your guide is loading game onto a horse or pack mule. Packing elk quarters is difficult and requires skill as well as brawn. It's fine to help but only if your guide asks you to.

Horses are like people—they have their own peculiarities. Here are some types with bad habits you're apt to meet up with, and suggestions on how to deal with them. Remember that a horse may try to get away with anything it can. It's up to you to show it that you're the boss and won't stand for any nonsense.

Ol' Plodder is a slow walker, so slow he'll leave you behind the group or cause a big gap in the string. To keep Plodder in step with the other horses, give him a smart rap with your boot heels when he drops behind. You won't hurt him, and you'll make him aware that he needs to move along. If your heels don't work, persuade him with a small branch. Give him a whack on his flanks as required. You don't need to use a baseball bat, just a small stick.

Ol' Trailshunner has a mind of his own and often refuses to follow the horses ahead along the trail. Use the reins whenever necessary, and keep him in line. Don't let him wander about to pick his own way if you're on a designated trail. He could lead you into a blowdown or obstacle course and cause problems.

Ol' Treehugger walks close to trees and seems intent on brushing you off his back. When he gets close to a tree, rein him widely away from it. If you have no choice but to brush by closely, gently stiff-arm the tree and ease the horse away from it.

Horses require food, water, and care, but they're valuable assets on an elk hunt. D.J. Reynolds and Steve Oldroyd, two of the author's hunting companions, water their horses before heading into the mountains.

Ol' Jumper loves to bound over logs in the trail. He'll bunch his feet and sail into the air, requiring you to hold on tightly. That's all you can do, other than cuss a lot. If you're unwilling to be a participant in this aerial maneuver, dismount and step over the log. Remount after Jumper does his thing.

Ol' Scarecrow is afraid of his shadow and will bolt at objects along the trail. A white chunk of fungus, a rock, or a grouse might make him rear back. If he does this often enough and it unnerves you, request another horse when you can.

Ol' Dancer is fidgety and doesn't like standing still. He acts nervous and waltzes around in camp while you're sitting on him, waiting to ride out with the group. As long as he doesn't demonstrate a rodeo act, about all you can do is put up with him until you start riding. He'll settle down as soon as you head down the trail.

Ol' Clumsy trips and stumbles a lot. This horse can be dangerous if he falls, so dismount and lead him across bad spots. When you get back to camp, tell the outfitter you'd just as soon ride a more surefooted beast for the duration of the hunt. Be aware, though, that horses trip and stumble as a matter of course. You should be concerned only if your horse is having a great deal more trouble than the others.

Horses need not be feared when you must hunt with them. If you'll use common sense and depend on your guide to help you along, a horse will be an asset. And don't be surprised if some of your fondest hunting memories involve horseback hunts. Mine do, and I intend to ride atop plenty more trusty steeds before calling it quits.

CHAPTER 21

Getting Your Elk Out

There are two ways to get your elk out of the woods: the easy way and the hard way.

The easy way is to tip the animal over next to a road and load it in your rig with four or five husky buddies. Another easy way is to hunt with an outfitter and let him or his guides do all the work of packing it out.

The hard way involves neither of the above.

It's pretty easy to sit in your living room on a sofa and plan an elk hunt and not consider the pitfalls that go with the hunt. After all, hauling a carcass out of the woods is something that you worry about if and when you are actually confronted with the situation. So you plan the hunt and figure that you'll deal with the heavy stuff when it happens.

Let's look at the heavy stuff. If your bullet or arrow or muzzleloader ball does its job, you will peer down at a mass of meat, bones, fur, innards, and antlers. The task at hand is to separate those items and transport the meat out of the boonies (and the fur and antlers if you want them).

You will have in front of you a lifeless animal that can weigh up to 1,000 pounds or more. Roll up your sleeves, get out your tools, and start right in.

At this point, let me list the tools you should have to process your elk in the woods:

Sturdy rope (about 50 feet)

Knife

Sharpening stone

Saw

Hatchet or hand ax

Lightweight block and tackle (optional but worthwhile)

Meat sacks

First, of course, be sure you fill out your permit in accordance with state regulations.

Next you'll need to field-dress the animal. Don't tarry; this job needs to be done immediately.

If the elk is lying on a steep slope, which is often the case, carefully tie a rope to his antlers, or around the neck if it's a cow, and fasten the other end snugly to a tree. If you don't, the animal could slide a considerable distance down the mountain and into a spot where you don't want it to be. This happened to me once, and now I secure the animal before I dress it.

Position the elk so you can get at its underside. If you're alone, this can be a major accomplishment. You'll probably have to push, pull, and shove to get it where you want it. I like to have the carcass lying on the back. At times I've tied the legs to trees to keep them spread apart and to steady the animal in one position.

With a sharp knife, start at the anus and work your way forward, cutting to one side of the testicles or udder. This cut should be made just under the skin. Continue it well up into the brisket, *only if you don't want to cape it out.* If you want the cape, end the cut well below the brisket.

Now that you have the skin parted up the middle of the underside, make a deeper cut along the same line, but guide the knife between two fingers, which also should be pushing in on the intestines and stomach so you don't puncture them.

As you cut, the innards will begin oozing out. Don't worry; keep cutting. When you're done, pull the intestines and stomach out slowly, severing the muscles and tissues that hold them in the cavity. Take care not to cut into the bladder, which lies just forward of the pelvic bone. This is the bone that runs crosswise between the hindquarters.

With most of the innards outside, carefully saw the pelvic bone up the middle, and cut and saw the meat and bone through to the anus. Carefully ream the anus and cut away the large intestine that leads to it. Carefully pull away the intestine, bladder and rest of the innards, taking care that fecal material doesn't drop into the cavity.

Note that I use the word "carefully" a lot. There's a good reason. If you puncture the bladder, urine will leak out into the meat. This is not good. Enough said.

With this chore at the lower end of the carcass completed, turn your attention to the upper section. You'll notice that forward of the diaphragm there are lots of organs such as the liver, heart and lungs. Pull them out slowly, again cutting any connective tissue that holds them in the cavity. When they're a good ways out, reach as far as you can up into the forward part of the chest and sever the esophagus. Pull it down, cutting as required, and the organs should soon be free of the carcass. Place the heart and liver in a clean spot, because you'll want to save them. Don't throw away the heart! It's absolutely delicious.

There will probably be a pool of blood in the cavity. If you can, maneuver the carcass so that this blood will drain away.

That was the easy part. Now you need to peel the hide and then cut the elk into quarters, unless you want to bone it on the spot.

To skin the carcass, make a slit underneath each hind-quarter from the anus area to the hock of each leg. To make the job easier, saw off each leg at the joint, or simply cut the leg off with a knife if you know how. If you find the correct joint with your knife blade, the leg will easily tear off without using a saw. Continue the process until you reach the front legs. Cut them off at the hocks, and make a cut underneath from the end of the leg to the original cut you made up the brisket. Keep skinning up to the neck. Remember: If you want the animal's cape, don't skin too high. See the diagram in the chapter on trophies for detailed instructions.

The skinning job will be a great deal easier if you can get the carcass up into the air. If you have a block and tackle, you can raise the hindquarters just far enough off the ground so you can work. As you progress, you can raise the carcass higher until you're done.

Most folks skin the elk on the ground. Start on one side; when you're done roll the animal carefully over on the loose skin to protect it from twigs, leaves and dirt, and start on the other side. Always allow the carcass to rest on the skin. You'll get plenty of forest debris on it no matter what you do, but it's best to keep it to a minimum.

With a skinned carcass before you, the next assignment is to cut it into pieces. Typically you'll cut it into four sections, but I cut them into five. Instead of sectioning the carcass all the way up the middle to the throat, I cut off the neck at the shoulders. On a mature elk, the neck will weigh 20 pounds or more. It's easier to handle in one piece and lightens the front quarters considerably when it's detached.

A word about skinning the neck: You'll find that it's the toughest part to peel away. The skin in this area doesn't rip off as the rest of the hide does, but must be cut bit by bit. This is a tedious job, but don't delay it. The fur is extemely thick here, and the meat will not cool adequately if not skinned immediately.

That brings to mind an Idaho hunt with outfitter Bruce Scott. I killed a big bull in the late afternoon and it took us until dark to dress it. We left it unskinned because we had a long uphill hike to our horses and a two-hour ride back to camp. We returned the next morning and immediately set about skinning and quartering the bull. Despite nighttime temperatures that were in the low 20's, the neck meat was still warm and on the verge of spoiling. Another few hours and the neck would have been fit for coyotes and ravens.

To quarter an elk, you can cut it down the entire length of the backbone which results in two halves. Then you cut the hindquarters off at the point where they join the body. Another way is to cut both hindquarters off first, and then cut both halves down the middle.

You'll soon find out that the task of cutting down the backbone is quite an ordeal. This is hard work, and you'll probably cuss whatever tool you're using.

You can use a saw, hatchet, or ax. The latter is quickest and easiest, but it's bulky to carry unless you've packed it on a horse. Furthermore, if you aren't a fair hand with an ax, you'll chop into a lot of meat. It's also tricky to use an ax alone because the halves should be spread as you chop. If a buddy is along to help, you need to be careful that you don't hurt him or her, because you'll be working in close quarters.

A hand ax is easier to use, but it doesn't deliver the power that an ax does. It's safer, and you can make more accurate strokes with it.

Most hunters I know use a compact saw that is carried on a belt holster. All well and good, but these tools are instruments of torture. After the first two minutes you'll be sweating like a demon and your arm muscles and lungs will protest violently. You'll swear an elk's bones are composed of high-alloy steel.

Lately I've seen outfitters and guides use a small tree pruning saw with a curved blade that folds into the handle. I've tried one, and it's the slickest saw I've seen.

With your elk in quarters, you should hang them in the shade of a tree unless you're going to load them immediately. A block and tackle will help hoist them up, or a husky pal will do nicely. Remember that each quarter of a big elk will weigh close to 100 pounds. If bears are about, hang the quarters on springy branches a few yards from the tree bole if you can. If you're worried about coyotes, hang the quarters at least three feet off the ground, six feet up or more for bears.

Wrap each quarter in a meat sack or cheesecloth to protect it from flies and birds such as ravens, whiskeyjacks and magpies. They can be a nuisance and make off with much of your meat or render it inedible. To insure that coyotes won't pay a visit to your meat while you're off getting help to haul it out, walk about 20 yards away from the hanging meat and purposely make a nature's call on several bushes in a wide circle. Sounds a mite uncivilized, but it works.

If you're built like a pro football linebacker, you might be able to haul a quarter out on your back. That's a mighty big project, and you'll need to be in fine form to do it. A packframe will do nicely to carry it.

For an idea of what it's like to haul out a quarter, lift a 92-pound sack of cement on your back and carry it over fallen logs, through thick brush, up a steep slope, across a slippery creek, over more fallen logs, and up more steep hills. No fair carrying the cement on the level. You won't be simulating elk country if you do.

If you must haul the meat out without assistance from a horse, you can eliminate 25 percent or more of the weight by boning it on the spot. Use a long-bladed knife to bone it with, and simply cut away big chunks. A rucksack will accommodate plenty of meat, or you can pack it in the pockets of your backpack.

I've packed out plenty of meat on my back, and I don't ever want to do it again. But I suppose I will, because there are places I hunt where a horse can't go.

Ah, a horse. That's the answer, the only answer, unless you can kill your elk near a road or a place where you can easily drive to it.

If you backpack or hunt without a horse, you'll have to bone your elk and carry it out pieces at a time.

But there are horses that will pack out an elk and act quite decently about the whole program, and there are horses that will have absolutely nothing to do with an elk. The latter will snort, balk, buck, rear back, kick like the devil, or a combination of those things. The latter horse is as good as no horse, and you're better off leaving the beast in the pasture or back at camp.

If you have a horse that will cooperate, you're only half-way through the chore of getting the meat out, because a horse can pack only half an elk. So you'll need two horses or have to make two trips. Maximum dead weight for a horse to pack is 200 to 250 pounds. That might seem light, but there's a world of difference between live and dead weight. A person will shift his body naturally to balance the weight as a horse climbs and descends mountains, but of course a load of meat or supplies just sits there.

There are a number of ways to pack out an elk. One technique is to cut the elk in half and lay it crosswise over the saddle. By making a slit in the carcass midway, the half is secured by slipping the saddle horn through the slit and lashing it down.

Another technique is to use a packsaddle. There are essentially two types: the sawbuck and Decker. The former is the most popular, perhaps because panniers can easily be slipped over the wooden crosspieces. Meat is loaded in the panniers and the whole works is tightly lashed down.

Panniers are simply containers that hold goods on a horse. They can be made of canvas, metal, wood, plastic, or other materials.

I can't stress enough the fact that packing a horse requires a great deal of skill. You won't learn it from this book, though I'll include some diagrams in this chapter to illustrate some of the basics. The only way to learn is to be out there in the firs and spruces with a partner who knows what he's doing and can teach you firsthand.

Besides knowing how to handle horses, you must understand knots. A good packer is a magician with ropes. I'm constantly impressed and am still learning, though I've been packing with my own horse for years.

Another important aspect of packing is balancing the load. Ten miles of rope and the best knots known to the Navy won't help if you don't know *exactly* how to balance the load and *make it stay there.* If you're lucky, you'll make it 50 yards up the trail with an unbalanced load before the whole works slips. Then you'll have to do it all over again.

I'll end this chapter with one last bit of advice. The reason for all the trouble and effort of getting your elk out is to ultimately offer it on the dinner table. That means you must make every attempt to keep the meat cold. If it's not cold enough and stays warm for too long, it will spoil, pure and simple. Remember: Dress the animal immediately and shuck the hide quickly. Cool those quarters and fuss over them as an old mother hen. They deserve your attention. Elk meat is superb, among the best meat you'll ever bring home from a hunting trip.

Appendix

State-by-State
Directory

The following information refers to states and Canadian provinces with major elk populations. Some states, such as Nevada, California, and eastern states with limited hunts have not been included. Special thanks to the Rocky Mountain Elk Foundation for information they provided.

ARIZONA

Don't let this arid southwest state fool you. Astute elk hunters know that Arizona has some of the biggest bulls in the West, and many are betting that the next world-record bull will come from this state. Since 1970, Arizona ranks third for elk in the Boone and Crockett and Pope and Young record books.

Despite Arizona's popularity as a desert region, almost 7,000 square miles of elk habitat can be found here, and the Fort Apache and San Carlos Indian reservations contribute

an enormous amount of elk country as well. About 80 percent of the elk habitat is on national forests. The total elk
population, including herds on Indian reservations, numbers
about 20,000. The bulk of the elk country is in the region
from Flagstaff along the Mogollon Rim to the New Mexico
border.

During the last 10 years, an average of 5,900 firearms
hunters on non-Indian lands harvested an average of 1,250
elk, or 12 percent of the estimated population, annually. The
trend in elk harvest has been upward since 1968. Elk populations increased to their peak in recent years in the Flagstaff area, but they continue to increase in the White
Mountains of eastern Arizona.

Hunters must apply for elk tags in a lottery that has a
late June application deadline. The regular elk hunt runs
from late November to early December.

For information on hunting regulations, contact the Arizona Game and Fish Department, 2222 W. Greenway Road,
Phoenix, AZ 85023 (602/942-3000).

National Forests:

Apache-Sitgreaves National Forest, Federal Bldg., P.O.
Box 640, Springervillè, AZ 85938 (602/333-4301).

Coconino National Forest, 2323 E. Greenlaw Lane,
Flagstaff, AZ 86001 (602/779-3311).

Coronado National Forest, 301 W. Congress, P.O. Box
551, Tucson, AZ 85702 (602/792-6483).

Kaibab National Forest, 800 S. Sixth St., Williams, AZ
86046 (602/635-2681).

Prescott National Forest, 344 S. Cortez, P.O. Box 2549,
Prescott, AZ 86031 (602/445-1762).

Tonto National Forest, 102 S. 28th St., P.O. Box 29070,
Phoenix, AZ 85038 (602/261-3205).

Bureau of Land Management: Arizona State Office,
2400 Valley Bank Center, Phoenix, AZ 85073 (602/261-
3873).

COLORADO

This is the top elk state in terms of populations, number of elk hunters, and harvest. About 200,000 hunters take some 30,000 elk annually.

The world record bull was killed in Colorado before the turn of the century, but the days of record-class bulls in Colorado seem to be gone forever. However, a new quality hunting program might turn this dismal picture around. Of late, 20 units were set aside that restrict the number of hunters. Quotas are set in each unit, and permits must be obtained in a lottery.

Unlimited numbers of licenses and easy access to much of Colorado's elk country is often blamed for the abundance of small bulls and poor bull-to-cow ratio.

All of western Colorado is elk country, with the exception of agricultural regions. Much of the area is national forest, with plenty of public access.

Colorado offers two general hunts of 11 days each. The first hunt starts in mid-October; the second begins in early November. Hunters can participate in only one season. The latter hunt is combined with the deer season; the first is for elk only.

The early season has an advantage because elk are relatively undisturbed, except by bow and black-powder hunters. Spike bulls are numerous and make up a large part of the harvest.

The later hunt allows hunters a good opportunity if heavy snow drives elk out of the high country and into lower regions accessible to hunters.

For a big bull, your best chances are in the backcountry if you hunt during the general season. Good bulls are taken from most of Colorado's national forests, but some of the best hunting is on private land. Expect to find crowded conditions on public land where there is good access.

Practically every private ranch is leased in Colorado. It's very difficult to obtain hunting permission on private lands in prime elk country.

For information on hunting regulations, contact the Colorado Division of Wildlife, 6060 Broadway, Denver, CO 80216 (303/297-1192).

National Forests:

Arapaho and Roosevelt National Forests, Federal Bldg., 301 S. Howes, Fort Collins, CO 80521 (303/482-5155).

Grand Mesa, Uncompahgre, and Gunnison National Forests, 11th and Main St., P.O. Box 138, Delta, CO 81416 (303/874-7691).

Pike and San Isabel National Forests, 910 Highway 50 West, Pueblo, CO 81008 (303/544-5277).

Rio Grande National Forest, 1803 W. Highway 160, Monte Vista, CO 81144 (303/852-5941).

Routt National Forest, Hunt Bldg., Steamboat Springs, CO 80477 (303/879-1722).

San Juan National Forest, Federal Bldg., 701 Camino Del Rio, Durango, CO 81301 (303/247-4874).

White River National Forest, Old Federal Bldg., Box 948, Glenwood Springs, CO 81601 (303/945-6582).

Bureau of Land Management: Colorado State Office, Colorado State Bank Bldg., 1600 Broadway, Denver, CO 80202 (303/837-4325).

IDAHO

A growing elk population is quickly putting Idaho back in the ranks with other top elk states. Hunters are taking an excess of 10,000 elk annually, and the prognosis for the future is bright. About 100,000 elk currently dwell in Idaho.

All of the state's mountainous regions have elk. National forests in the Panhandle and region along and south of the Salmon River have good elk herds.

Several wilderness areas in Idaho offer excellent hunting. The Selway Wilderness, one of the biggest in North

America, has some big bulls and offers an early general firearms season.

The statewide general elk hunt starts in October, but dates vary with the units.

Idaho ranks high in the Boone and Crockett record book for record-class bulls and will likely produce more trophy heads in the future.

The Panhandle region has some thickly timbered forests, among the densest in the Rockies. Elk are tough to find in the heavy cover, but persistent hunters do well every year. Cows are often legal game in the Panhandle.

Resident tags are unlimited; nonresidents must obtain a license on a first-come basis. In recent years the nonresident quota has been selling out rapidly.

For information on hunting regulations, contact the Idaho Department of Fish and Game, 600 S. Walnut, P.O. Box 25, Boise, ID 83707 (208/334-3700).

National Forests:

Boise National Forest, 1075 Park Blvd., Boise, ID 83706 (208/334-1516).

Caribou National Forest, 250 S. Fourth Ave., Pocatello, ID 83201 (208/232-1142).

Challis National Forest, Forest Service Bldg., Challis, ID 83226 (208/879-2285).

Clearwater National Forest, Rt. 4, Orofino, ID 83544 (208/476-4541).

Idaho Panhandle National Forest, 1201 Ironwood Drive, Couer d'Alene, ID 83814 (208/667-2561).

Nezperce National Forest, 319 E. Main St., Grangeville, ID 83530 (208/983-1950).

Payette National Forest, Forest Service Bldg., P.O. Box 1026, McCall, ID 83638 (208/634-2255).

Salmon National Forest, Forest Service Bldg., Salmon, ID 83467 (208/756-2215).

Sawtooth National Forest, 1525 Addison Ave. East,

Twin Falls, ID 83301 (208/733-3698).

Targhee National Forest, 420 N. Bridge St., St. Anthony, ID 83455 (208/624-3151).

Bureau of Land Management: Idaho State Office, 398 Federal Bldg., 550 W. Fort St., Boise, ID 83724 (208/384-1401).

MONTANA

The biggest of our Rocky Mountain states has a fine elk population, with an estimated 100,000 animals. Montana has the distinction of producing more Boone and Crockett trophy-class elk than any other state, with 61 heads listed in the current edition of the book.

Western Montana's mountain ranges are home to the elk, although there are some excellent herds in isolated areas east of the mountains. The C.M. Russell Wildlife Refuge offers a fine hunt annually, but there is plenty of competition for the lottery-drawn permits.

Big bulls are killed everywhere in Montana's mountains, but some of the biggest are consistently taken from the Yellowstone Park region. Two units, the Gallatin and Gardiner, offer very late hunts that run from early December to late February. A lottery draw is required to obtain a tag. In both areas, elk migrating out of Yellowstone Park are hunted during the two- and four-day seasons.

Several national forests provide excellent hunting. The huge Bob Marshall Wilderness has plenty of elk, and the wilderness as well as areas adjacent to Yellowstone offer an early general gun season.

The statewide general season begins in late October and runs into late November, allowing five weeks of hunting.

Resident tags are unlimited, but nonresidents must buy a tag on a first-come basis. The quota sells out quickly, as soon as the licenses go on sale. Nonresidents must purchase a combination elk license, which is also good for deer, black bear, birds, and fishing.

For information on hunting regulations, contact the Montana Division of Fish, Wildlife, and Parks, 1420 E. Sixth Ave., Helena, MT 59601.

National Forests:

Beaverhead National Forest, P.O. Box 1258, Dillon, MT 59725 (406/683-2312).

Bitterroot National Forest, 316 N. Third St., Hamilton, MT 59840 (406/363-3131).

Custer National Forest, P.O. Box 2556, Billings, MT 59103 (406/657-6361).

Deerlodge National Forest, Federal Bldg., P.O. Box 400, Butte, MT 59701 (406/723-6561).

Flathead National Forest, P.O. Box 147, 290 N. Main, Kalispell, MT 59901 (406/755-5401).

Gallatin National Forest, Federal Bldg., P.O. Box 130, Bozeman, MT 59715 (406/587-5271).

Helena National Forest, Federal Bldg., Drawer 10014, Helena MT 59601 (406/449-5201).

Kootenai National Forest, W. Highway 2, Libby, MT 59923 (406/293-6211).

Lewis and Clark National Forest, Federal Bldg., Great Falls, MT 59403 (406/453-7678).

Bureau of Land Management: Montana State Office, 222 N. 32nd St., P.O. Box 30157, Billings, MT 59107 (406/657-6462).

NEW MEXICO

This southwest state has a healthy population of elk and annually gives up some very large bulls. This is the state that has the extensive private tracts that offer quality hunting to hunters who want a big bull without the pack-in backcountry-type trip. Those hunts are comparatively expensive, but hunter success is extremely high, often better than 90 percent on some ranches. These are wild elk, not fenced animals that might be found in preserves.

The chapter on southwest elk gives details about the private holdings, along with addresses and telephone numbers.

About 30,000 elk live in New Mexico, with an annual harvest of about 2,500 animals.

Beside the ranches, some Indian reservations have very good elk hunting, but prices are high as well. Some good bulls are killed on the tribal lands, with a very high hunter success rate.

National forests provide good elk hunting in New Mexico, especially in the northern half of the state. Part of the famous Vermejo Ranch was given to the U.S. Forest Service recently. It is now managed by the state wildlife department as a quality area.

Elk seasons vary with the unit, starting in October. Usually there are five different hunts, each less than one week long. A hunter may hunt only one season.

Tags for public land are issued in a lottery to residents and nonresidents alike. On private lands, landowners may distribute a quota of tags as they wish.

For information on hunting regulations, contact the New Mexico Game and Fish Department, Villagra Bldg., Santa Fe, NM 87503 (505/827-7899).

National Forests:

Carson National Forest, Forest Service Bldg., P.O. Box 558, Taos, NM 87571 (505/758-2238).

Cibola National Forest, 10308 Candelaria NE, Albuquerque, NM 87112 (505/766-2185).

Gila National Forest, 2610 N. Silver St., Silver City, NM 88061 (505/388-1986).

Lincoln National Forest, Federal Bldg., llth and New York, Alamogordo, NM 88310 (505/437-6030).

Santa Fe National Forest, Federal Bldg., Box 1689, Santa Fe, NM 87501 (505/988-6328).

Bureau of Land Management: New Mexico State Office, Federal Bldg., South Federal Place, Santa Fe, NM 87501 (505/988-6217).

OREGON

Both subspecies of elk, the Roosevelt's and Rocky Mountain, live in Oregon. The Roosevelt's elk inhabits the Cascade Mountains west to the Coast Range, and Rocky Mountain elk occupy the region in eastern Oregon.

About 100,000 elk are estimated to live in Oregon, about 60 percent of them the Rocky Mountain subspecies.

Roosevelt's elk dwell in extremely dense rain forests. Hunting is done by watching openings from log decks or clearcut areas, or sneaking through the very heavy timber. Several national forests and private paper companies offer hunting opportunities in both western and eastern Oregon.

Trophy hunters should try the Snake River, Minam, and Imnaha units in the northeast for big bulls. There may be a minimum-size antler restriction in these quality areas.

On the west side, trophy hunters can try the Tioga Unit in the southwest and the Saddle Mountain Unit in the northwest. There are also minimum size antler restrictions in these units.

Oregon often ranks second only to Colorado in terms of numbers of elk harvested, with more than 15,000 usually taken each season. Most elk killed are the Rocky Mountain subspecies.

Elk tags are unrestricted for residents and nonresidents. Seasons for Rocky Mountain elk usually start in October; Roosevelt's elk seasons start in November.

For information on hunting regulations, contact the Oregon Department of Fish and Wildlife, P.O. Box 3503, Portland, OR 97208 (503/229-5551).

National Forests:

Deschutes National Forest, 211 NE Revere Ave., Bend, OR 97701 (503/382-6922).

Fremont National Forest, 34 North D St., Lakeview, OR 97630 (503/947-2151).

Malheur National Forest, 139 NE Dayton St., John Day, OR 97845 (503/575-1731).

Mt. Hood National Forest, 2440 SE 195th, Portland, OR 97233 (503/667-0511).

Ochoco National Forest, Federal Bldg., Prineville, OR 97754 (503/447-6247).

Rogue River National Forest, Federal Bldg., 333 W. Eighth St., P.O. Box 520, Medford, OR 97501 (503/779-2351).

Siskiyou National Forest, P.O. Box 440, Grants Pass, OR 97526 (503/479-5301).

Siuslaw National Forest, P.O. Box 1148, Corvallis, OR 97330 (503/757-4480).

Umatilla National Forest, 2517 SW Hailey Ave., Pendleton, OR 97801 (503/276-3811).

Umpqua National Forest, Federal Office Bldg., Roseburg, OR 97470 (503/672-6601).

Wallowa and Whitman National Forests, Federal Office Bldg., P.O. Box 907, Baker, OR 97814 (503/523-6391).

Willamette National Forest, 211 E. Seventh Ave., Eugene, OR 97440 (503/687-6533).

Winema National Forest, P.O. Box 1390, Klamath Falls, OR 97601 (503/882-7761).

Bureau of Land Management: 729 NE Oregon St., P.O. Box 2965, Portland, OR 97208 (503/234-4001).

UTAH

Elk herds are scattered around Utah; most of them are in the north and northeast regions. A herd of about 25,000 lives in the state, with about 4,000 killed annually.

Utah has never produced an official record-class elk, but some good bulls are taken each year from scattered areas. The best hunting is in restricted units that require a lottery draw for a tag.

Transplanted herds in the south and central regions are growing rapidly and are giving up nice bulls. One of the best is the Book Cliffs herd in the northeast. Hunters who draw a permit here have an excellent chance of taking a fine, mature bull.

The High Uintas Primitive Area in the northern region offers backcountry hunting to sportsmen who are prepared to penetrate this large, remote region.

Utah's biggest elk dwell on the Ute Indian reservations, but nontribal members have not been allowed to hunt it for years. If that changes, the area will likely produce a record-class head.

The general elk season starts in early October and runs for two weeks. The season coincides with the rut, but heavy pressure from hunters and plenty of easy access often stymie hunters who try to bugle bulls.

Permits are unrestricted but must be purchased prior to a late summer cutoff date.

For information on hunting regulations, contact the Utah Division of Wildlife Resources, 1596 W. North Temple, Salt Lake City, UT 84116 (801/533-9333).

National Forests:

Ashley National Forest, 437 E. Main St., Vernal, UT 84078 (801/789-1181).

Dixie National Forest, 82 N. 100 E. St., Cedar City, UT 84720 (801/586-2421).

Fishlake National Forest, 170 N. Main St., Richfield, UT 84701 (801/896-4491).

Manti-Lasal National Forest, 599 West 100 South, Price, UT 84501 (801/637-2817).

Uinta National Forest, 88 West 1 North, Provo, UT 84601 (801/584-9101).

Wasatch National Forest, 8226 Federal Bldg., 125 S. State St., Salt Lake City, UT 84138 (801/524-5030).

Bureau of Land Management: Utah State Office, University Club Bldg., 136 South Temple, Salt Lake City, UT 84111 (801/524-5311).

WASHINGTON

This state has areas of very heavy timber and has an excellent and thriving elk population. The Roosevelt's subspecies occupies the forests of the Cascade Mountains west to the Coast forests. The Rocky Mountain elk lives in the eastern regions, in mountain ranges that have very good elk habitat.

National forests provide plenty of good public hunting in both regions, and a wealth of private paper companies allow hunting on much of their lands.

The Rocky Mountain subspecies is the most popular in Washington, perhaps because it lives in more open landscape and has larger antlers. Roosevelt's elk are bigger in body stature, but they're extemely difficult to hunt in the dense western forests.

About 60,000 elk live in Washington, with about 35,000 being the Roosevelt's subspecies and 25,000 the Rocky Mountain subspecies. The average annual harvest for both species runs about 10,000.

Season dates vary, depending on the region, and there are some excellent quality units with varying dates as well. The quality areas offer a superb opportunity for a nice bull, and hunter success rates are much higher than the statewide average.

Licenses are unlimited to residents and nonresidents. For information on hunting conditions, contact the Washington Game Department, 600 N. Capitol Way, Olympia, WA 98504 (206/753-5700).

National Forests:

Colville National Forest, Colville, WA 99114 (509/684-5221).

Gifford Pinchot National Forest, 500 W. 12th St., Vancouver, WA 98660 (206/696-4041).

Mt. Baker and Snoqualmie National Forests, 1601 Second Ave., Seattle, WA 98101 (206/442-5400).

Okanogan National Forest, 1240 Second Ave. S., Okanogan, WA 98840 (509/422-2704).

Olympia National Forest, P.O. Box 2288, Olympia, WA 98507 (206/753-9534).

Wenatchee National Forest, 301 Yakima St., Wenatchee, WA 98801 (509/662-4323).

Bureau of Land Management: 729 NE Oregon St., P.O. Box 2965, Portland, OR 97208 (503/234-4001).

WYOMING

Most elk populations are in the western mountains of Wyoming, with large concentrations in Yellowstone National Park, Teton National Park, and adjacent national forests. The Shoshone and Bridger-Teton National forests are popular areas for elk in the western region. In the south-central area, the Medicine Bow National Forest has good elk hunting. The Bighorn National Forest in the north-central region is well known for elk.

A unique elk hunt is held in the Red Desert each year.

Hunters seek elk in low elevations, most of it sagebrush and prairie. This and other quality hunts like it offer elk hunting to sportsmen who win tags in a lottery. Special late hunts are held annually in Teton National Park and the National Elk Refuge.

Wyoming's biggest elk come from scattered locations, but the Wyoming Range in the Bridger-Teton National Park is one of the best spots. The Shoshone National Forest east of Yellowstone Park is also a fine spot for big bulls.

Elk season normally begins October 1 or 15, depending on the unit, but dates vary in others. Some early backcountry hunts are held in September. They occur during the rut and are superb hunts for taking big bulls.

Residents obtain general licenses on an unlimited basis; nonresidents must apply for a tag each year with an application deadline of February 1. About 7,000 tags are available to nonresidents.

During a typical year, 55,000 hunters pursue elk, with an annual harvest of about 15,000. Wyoming's elk herd numbers about 80,000 animals.

For information on hunting regulations, write the Wyoming Game and Fish Department, Cheyenne, WY 82002.

National Forests:

Bridger-Teton National Forest, Forest Service Bldg., Jackson, WY 83001 (307/733-2752).

Bighorn National Forest, Columbus Bldg., P.O. Box 2046, Sheridan, WY 82801 (307/672-2457).

Medicine Bow National Forest, 605 Skyline Drive, Laramie, WY 82070 (307/745-8971).

Shoshone National Forest, West Yellowstone Highway, P.O. Box 2140, Cody, WY 82414 (307/587-2274).

Bureau of Land Management: Wyoming State Office, 2515 Warren Ave., P.O. Box 1828, Cheyenne, WY 82001 (307/778-2326).

ALBERTA

There is a fine elk herd in this Canadian province, including some enormous bulls. It is interesting to note that the biggest elk of the 20th century was killed in Alberta in 1977.

Alberta once had an elk population of about 30,000 animals, but excessive crop damage and competition with livestock led to a reduction in the mid-1960's and early 1970's. Currently, a healthy herd of about 18,000 exists. Hunters harvest about 2,000 elk annually.

Elk are found in four major habitat types. They include subalpine, boreal mixed woods, boreal uplands, and boreal foothills.

During a typical season, elk are hunted in seven rifle zones, of which two zones are designated as trophy areas. These two zones include nearly all of the east slopes of the Rocky Mountains north of and including the Highwood Range. A trophy elk is defined as a male elk bearing antlers, one of which has a main beam from which projects no less than four tines not less than three inches in length.

For information on hunting regulations, contact the Alberta Fish and Wildlife Division, Petroleum Plaza Bldg., Edmonton, Alberta, Canada T5H 2C9 (403/427-6749).

BRITISH COLUMBIA

There is a healthy population of about 27,000 elk in British Columbia. The harvest runs about 3,000 annually, and some excellent bulls are killed.

Roosevelt's elk occur on Vancouver Island and occasionally find their way to the lower mainland from Washington State. Rocky Mountain elk occur mainly in the Kootenays (the Rocky, Purcell, Selkirk, and Monashee mountain

ranges) and farther north (Omineca-Peace Resource Management Region) in the lower Peace River area (the Murray-
Wapiti River drainages) and the Muskwa-Prophet River
drainages on the eastern slope of the Rocky Mountains.

For information on hunting regulations, contact the
British Columbia Fish and Wildlife Branch, Parliament
Bldgs., Victoria, British Columbia, Canada V8V 1X4 (604/
387-6409).

Index

253